Quick Guide

FENCES & GATES

CREATIVE HOMEOWNER PRESS®

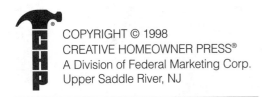

COPYRIGHT © 1998
CREATIVE HOMEOWNER PRESS®
A Division of Federal Marketing Corp.
Upper Saddle River, NJ

Quick Guide is a registered trademark of Creative Homeowner Press®

Manufactured in the United States of America

Editorial Director: Timothy O. Bakke
Art Director: Annie Jeon

Author: Jim Barrett
Editor: Jeff Day
Editorial Assistant: Albert Huang
Copyeditor: Margaret Gallos

Graphic Designers: Melisa DelSordo, Jan Greco, John Larimer
Illustrators: Ray Skibinski, Craig Franklin, Paul M. Schumm
Cover Design: Warren Ramezzana
Cover Illustrations: Vincent Alessi

Electronic Prepress and Printing:
Command Web Offset, Inc.

Current Printing (last digit)
10 9 8 7 6 5 4 3 2 1

Quick Guide: Fences & Gates
Library of Congress Catalog Card Number: 97-075265
ISBN: 1-58011-007-X

CREATIVE HOMEOWNER PRESS®
A Division of Federal Marketing Corp.
24 Park Way
Upper Saddle River, NJ 07458

C O N T E N T S

Getting Started   5

Setting Posts   11

Building the Fence   23

Installing Metal & Vinyl Fences   47

Building & Installing Gates   57

Maintaining & Repairing Fences   69

Glossary   79

Index   80

Though all the designs and methods in this book have been tested for safety, it is not possible to overstate the importance of using the safest construction methods possible. What follows are reminders; some do's and don'ts of basic carpentry. They are not substitutes for your own common sense.

- *Always* use caution, care, and good judgment when following the procedures described in this book.

- *Always* be sure that the electrical setup is safe; be sure that no circuit is overloaded and that all power tools and electrical outlets are properly grounded. Do not use power tools in wet locations.

- *Always* read container labels on paints, solvents, and other products; provide ventilation, and observe all other warnings.

- *Always* read the manufacturer's instructions for using a tool, especially the warnings.

- *Always* use hold-downs and push sticks whenever possible when working on a table saw. Avoid working short pieces if you can.

- *Always* remove the key from any drill chuck (portable or press) before starting the drill.

- *Always* pay deliberate attention to how a tool works so that you can avoid being injured.

- *Always* know the limitations of your tools. Do not try to force them to do what they were not designed to do.

- *Always* make sure that any adjustment is locked before proceeding. For example, always check the rip fence on a table saw or the bevel adjustment on a portable saw before starting to work.

- *Always* clamp small pieces firmly to a bench or other work surface when using a power tool on them.

- *Always* wear the appropriate work gloves when handling chemicals, moving or stacking lumber, or doing heavy construction.

- *Always* wear a disposable face mask when you create dust by sawing or sanding. Use a special filtering respirator when working with toxic substances and solvents.

- *Always* wear eye protection, especially when using power tools or striking metal on metal or concrete; a chip can fly off, for example, when chiseling concrete.

- *Always* be aware that there is seldom enough time for your body's reflexes to save you from injury from a power tool in a dangerous situation; everything happens too fast. Be *alert!*

- *Always* keep your hands away from the business ends of blades, cutters, and bits.

- *Always* hold a circular saw firmly, usually with both hands so that you know where they are.

- *Always* use a drill with an auxiliary handle to control the torque when large-size bits are used.

- *Always* check your local building codes when planning new construction. The codes are intended to protect public safety and should be observed to the letter.

- *Never* work with power tools when you are tired or under the influence of alcohol or drugs.

- *Never* cut tiny pieces of wood or pipe using a power saw. Cut small pieces off larger pieces.

- *Never* change a saw blade or a drill or router bit unless the power cord is unplugged. Do not depend on the switch being off; you might accidentally hit it.

- *Never* work in insufficient lighting.

- *Never* work while wearing loose clothing, hanging hair, open cuffs, or jewelry.

- *Never* work with dull tools. Have them sharpened, or learn how to sharpen them yourself.

- *Never* use a power tool on a workpiece that is not firmly supported or clamped.

- *Never* saw a workpiece that spans a large distance between horses without close support on each side of the cut; the piece can bend, closing on and jamming the blade, causing saw kickback.

- *Never* support a workpiece with your leg or other part of your body when sawing.

- *Never* carry sharp or pointed tools, such as utility knives, awls, or chisels, in your pocket. If you want to carry such tools, use a special-purpose tool belt with leather pockets and holders.

GETTING STARTED

You'll have to choose the type and amount of lumber and related materials—fasteners, hardware, and concrete, to name a few—required to build the fence design you've chosen.

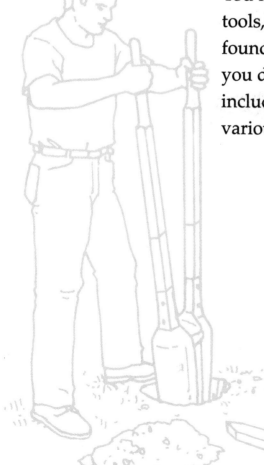

You'll need carpentry and digging tools. Most of these tools, such as shovels, hammers, and hand saws, are found in almost any home, and you can rent the tools you don't have from your local rental shop. Such tools include posthole diggers, portable cement mixers, various mason's tools, or paint spray rigs.

Layout & Digging Tools

To mark the fence line and determine the location of the fence posts, you'll need mason's twine (or sturdy, non-stretchable string), a 50- or 100-foot tape measure, a stick of red or other bright-colored chalk, a plumb bob, wooden stakes, and a mallet or hammer to drive the stakes. To lay out corners, extra stakes will be required to construct batter boards. (See "Plotting a Fence," page 12, for how to set up batter boards.)

Postholes generally need to be deep (usually at least 2½ feet) and narrow (about twice the width of the post; for 4x4 and 6x6 posts, that's about 8 to 12 inches in diameter). Digging such deep, narrow holes isn't easy with a shovel; instead, use a clamshell digger or hand auger. Clamshell diggers are better for hard or rocky soil; hand augers work best in loose or sandy soil. The depth of the postholes you'll be able to dig depends on the length of the tool's handles; generally, cheaper tools have shorter handles, so they dig smaller holes. If the soil is hard and rocky, you can use a modified clamshell digger with a lever that traps loose dirt, or you can use a pickaxe, a digging bar, or possibly a jackhammer to break up and remove the rocks. If you have a lot of holes to dig, it will be worthwhile to rent a power auger from a local tool rental shop. This tool works like a large, gasoline-powered drill for boring holes in the ground. One-person and two-person models are available. If you have a helper, you'll find the two-person model easier to operate.

If you're setting the posts in concrete, you'll need a hoe, shovel, and wheelbarrow or sheet of plywood for mixing concrete. Although you can mix some types of concrete directly in the posthole rather than in a wheelbarrow, you'll still need a wheelbarrow to transport the mix to the postholes.

Posts need to stand straight up and down, or plumb. You can plumb posts vertically with an ordinary 24-inch level, although the job will go faster if you use a special two-way post level like the one shown in the drawing "Fencing Tools." The level plumbs posts on two faces at once and is available at most large home centers and hardware stores. A line level and string come in handy for setting posts to the same height and determining rail locations on the posts. Or you might purchase an inexpensive water level—a clear plastic tube filled with colored water—to level the post tops and lay out rail locations.

Chain link fences require a few specialized tools, which can be purchased or rented at a rental shop or where you buy the chain link fencing.

Lumber

If you're building a fence, gate, or trellis of wood, one of the most important decisions you'll need to make is what type and quality of lumber you'll use. Lumber comes in a wide variety of sizes, shapes, grades, and surface textures. For the most part, your choices will be limited to what's readily available at local lumberyards and home centers. Price and quality can vary by quite a bit from store to store, so it's worthwhile to estimate the amounts you need and do some comparative shopping.

When buying fencing lumber, you'll have to make three separate, but integrated choices: what to use for the posts, what to use for the rails, and what to use for the siding, if any. Most wood fences use 4x4 or 6x6 posts and 2x4 rails. Wood siding may be boards, pickets, lath, or even plywood.

Decay Resistance

For a long fence life, choose a decay-resistant wood. Pressure-treated posts and rails are your best bet: They are widely available and typically cost less and last longer than naturally decay-resistant species, such as redwood or red cedar. Most treated lumber is preserved with chromated copper arsenate (CCA), which gives the wood its characteristic green or greenish-brown color. This type of treated lumber is easily stained. If left bare, the wood will eventually lose its green color and weather to a silvery gray.

CCA pressure-treated wood is rated for above-ground use or for contact with the ground, based on the amount of preservative injected into the wood. Lumber labeled 0.25—which means it contains preservative in a concenration of 0.25 pound per cubic foot (pcf)—should be used only above ground. For use in contact with the ground, buy lumber rated at 0.40 pcf. You can't always find lumber that's labeled, however, so ask at the lumberyard or home center whether the lumber is rated for ground contact.

Properly installed, pressure-treated posts and rails will last as long as 50 years, according to manufacturers. However, because the preservative does not always penetrate completely through the wood, you'll need to treat cut ends with a wood preservative. Orient posts with the uncut end down, and treat the top with preservative. You can buy wood preservatives under several common brand names in hardware stores and home centers; better preservative formulas also contain a water repellent. You can apply preservative by either brushing it on the end grain or soaking the ends of boards and posts in a container of preservative. When applying preservatives, wear heavy rubber gloves, long sleeves, goggles, and a respirator designed to filter mists and vapors.

The preservative in treated lumber will not easily leach out of the wood, so you do not need to worry about contamination of garden soil or plants from a few posts. However, the sawdust is toxic, so cut the lumber outdoors while wearing a dust mask.

Try Square

Tape Measure

Chalkline

T-Bevel

Water Level

Plumb Bob

Wrecking Bar

Posthole Digger

Power Auger

Combination Square

Angle Square

Framing Square

Level

Hammer

Chisel

Circular Saw

Block Plane

Power Miter Saw

Post Level

Goggles

Dust Mask

Saber Saw

Other types of wood preservatives include creosote and borate salts. Creosote should not be used because it is toxic to plants and animals. Borate-treated lumber is effective against carpenter ants, termites, and other wood-boring insects. But it has only limited effectiveness against fungus and mold.

Posts and rails made from decay-resistant species, such as redwood or cedar, often are used when appearance is a factor, say, when repeating house-siding materials in the fence. The surfaces of redwood and cedar posts and rails are either smooth (dressed) or rough-sawn for a rustic appearance.

Generally, untreated softwoods, such as fir, pine, spruce, or hemlock, should not be used for fences. If you do use these woods, keep them painted or stained with a stain-preservative to protect them from the elements. Never use these softwoods for posts or other members that come in contact with the ground.

Lumber Grades

When you go to the lumberyard, you'll discover that lumber comes in many different grades, usually identified by stamps on the lumber. The best grades are also the most expensive and probably inappropriate for fence construction. Lower grades have more defects, including knots, splits, bends, and even rot. A lot of lower grade lumber is perfectly acceptable for fence construction, but you'll have to dig through the stacks to find pieces with defects that you can live with or cut off.

You can't always rely on grade stamps alone. Lumberyards often mix grades when the lumber is restacked in the yard or may apply their own designations, such as premium, economy, decking, or garden grade. Also, lumber may not be properly stacked or stored, which results in twisting, warping, decay, or the growth of mildew. You can skirt all these problems by selecting your

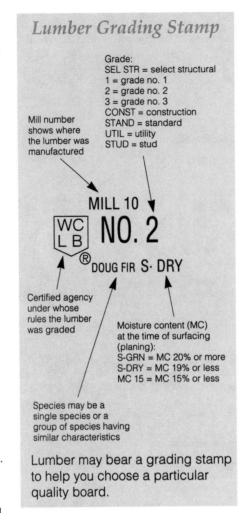

Lumber Grading Stamp

Mill number shows where the lumber was manufactured

Grade:
SEL STR = select structural
1 = grade no. 1
2 = grade no. 2
3 = grade no. 3
CONST = construction
STAND = standard
UTIL = utility
STUD = stud

MILL 10
WCLB NO. 2
® DOUG FIR S· DRY

Certified agency under whose rules the lumber was graded

Moisture content (MC) at the time of surfacing (planing):
S-GRN = MC 20% or more
S-DRY = MC 19% or less
MC 15 = MC 15% or less

Species may be a single species or a group of species having similar characteristics

Lumber may bear a grading stamp to help you choose a particular quality board.

lumber by hand. If you're using pressure-treated lumber, No. 1 grade is the best quality, followed by No. 2 grade and No. 3 grade. No. 2 grade is a good compromise between cost and quality.

Redwood Grades

The redwood trees of California and the Pacific Northwest are legendary for their size and the quality of the lumber they provide. Redwood's beautiful straight grain, natural glowing color, and weather resistance have traditionally marked it as the Cadillac of outdoor building materials.

You can usually tell sapwood from heartwood by color: the sapwood is lighter and hardly makes one think of *red* wood. Redwood heartwood is extremely weather- and insect-resistant, but the sapwood may start to rot in two or three years if it contacts the ground or remains wet for

long periods of time. Treat sapwood with a preservative, and use it only where the wood will be dry for most of the year.

You can let redwood go gray by not treating it with anything; it will reach a light gray color and a slight sheen that many people find attractive. Or you can treat it with stains and a U.V. blocker to keep it close to its original color.

Redwood grades are established by the Redwood Inspection Service of the California Redwood Association. Architectural grades are the best-looking and most expensive grades of redwood. Garden Grades are more economical and have more knots. Both categories of redwood are available kiln-dried or unseasoned and are usually surfaced on four sides.

Garden Grades of redwood are suitable for most fence-building applications. They include:

Construction Heart/Deck Heart. This is an all-heartwood grade containing knots. It is recommended for work on or near the ground, such as posts, beams, joists, and decking. It is the most expensive Garden-Grade redwood. Deck Heart looks the same as Construction Heart, but it is graded for strength so it can be used in deck construction. Deck Heart is available in 2x4 and 2x6 only and isn't really suited to fence work.

Construction Common/Deck Common. Any redwood grade that doesn't have heart in its name is a mixture of heart and sapwood. Construction and Deck Common are cheaper than their all-heart counterparts, but a board may contain noticeable differences in color. Other than that, Construction Common and Deck Common are identical to the Construction and Deck Heart. They cost less than heart. Construction Common is a good choice for fence rails.

Merchantable Heart. This is the most economical all-heartwood grade. It allows larger knots and smaller knot holes. It is suitable for fences and posts. It is the grade found in most prefabricated fencing.

Merchantable. This has the same characteristics as Merchantable Heart but contains sapwood. It is suitable for fence boards and trellises as well as above ground garden and utility applications. It is usually the least expensive grade available.

Architectural grades are more expensive than garden grades and include:

Clear All-Heart. All heartwood and free from knots, this wood is recommended for highly visible applications, and should be reserved for fancy, high-end fences.

Clear. Similar in quality to Clear All-Heart, expect that Clear contains sapwood. Clear is ideal for highly visible applications where the wood won't be subjected to rot.

B-Heart. Containing limited knots, but no sapwood, B-Heart is a less costly alternative to Clear All-Heart.

B-Grade. Similar characteristics to B-Heart, but contains sapwood; same uses as Clear.

Estimating & Ordering Lumber

Most lumberyards sell precut lumber by the running foot, typically in 24-inch increments. Precut fence boards are an exception; many are sold in 60-inch lengths. Lumber may also be sold by the board foot, especially if you're buying very large amounts. A board foot is equal to the amount of wood contained in a board 1 foot wide by 1 foot long by 1 inch thick. Remember that board-foot sizes are nominal, not actual, and are used for ordering purposes only. If the local lumberyard sells wood by the board foot, give the clerk your linear foot estimate, and he will convert it.

To help estimate the actual amount and lengths of posts, rails, and siding materials, measure the overall length of the fence line, then plot and mark the locations of the posts. To figure rail sizes and amounts, measure the distance between each post to get rail lengths. (If the rails will be set in mortised or dadoed posts, add the extra length to the rails.) Next, determine the number of fence sections needed, and multiply this figure by the number of rails in each section to get the total number of rails required.

To determine how many boards, pickets, or other siding pieces are required to cover one section, divide the length of the section by the actual width of the board or picket. Then, multiply this figure by the number of sections in the fence. Remember to use actual board widths in your calculations, not nominal widths. Buy one or two extra posts and rails and a few extra boards or pickets to allow for cutting errors. If you're using fancy pickets or trim pieces, order a few extra for future repairs.

To avoid wasting lumber, it's best to lay out the fence to take advantage of standard lengths. For example, you can space posts on 72- or 96-inch centers, rather than 60- or 84-inch centers. If you must use odd spacings, determine how to make best use of standard lengths. Plan your cuts to maximize wood use.

Codes & Ordinances

Before you get too far along with your plans, contact your local planning council or building department to see what building codes, zoning laws, and city ordinances affect the size, design, and location of the intended fence. Most urban and suburban communities have fence-height laws —typically a maximum of 72 inches for boundary fences in back and side yards, and 36 or 48 inches for fences bordering the street or sidewalk. In some communities, you may be able to exceed the maximum fence height if the top portion is made of wire, lattice, or other open work. If you can't exceed the limits you can use trees or shrubs to provide privacy.

In addition to height restrictions, codes may stipulate setbacks and easements, which require that structures be built a certain distance from the street, sidewalk or property line. This is especially true if you're erecting the fence on a corner lot, where it could create a blind corner at a street intersection or sharp bend in the road. Usually, front-yard fences more than 36 to 48 inches high must be set back a certain distance from the sidewalk; fences more than 72 inches high usually must be set back from side and rear property lines. Check local codes.

Never assume that other fences in your neighborhood meet local codes and ordinances. If you see a design that you particularly like, you might ask the owners if there are any plans for it or where they bought the materials. You might also ask permission to reproduce the design. However, before you begin construction, check that the design conforms with guidelines set by your building department. In some cases, you'll need to get a building permit and arrange for one or more building inspections.

Check to see if there are any neighborhood covenants or restrictions that govern the style of fence. In some neighborhoods, homeowners' associations have gained the legal right to dictate what type of structure you can erect, what materials you can use, and even what colors you can paint it. Such restrictions are designed to maintain the architectural character of the neighborhood. Also, if your house has some historical significance in the community or is in a neighborhood designated as a historical area, you may have to get your plans approved by a local architectural review board to make sure the fence design is appropriate.

If your plans conflict with local zoning ordinances, you can apply for a variance: a permit or waiver to build a structure that does not adhere strictly to local property use laws.

When you apply for the variance, there's usually a fee and often a public hearing where neighbors and others involved can express their opinions. When you present your plans to the zoning commission for review, you must prove to them that you have a valid reason for requesting the variance. Even if you go through the entire process, there's no guarantee that you will be granted a variance. It's a lot easier just to keep your design within the limits of local zoning laws.

Locating Utilities

Before you start digging postholes, you must know the exact locations and depth of underground utility

Locating Utilities. Before you dig postholes, ask the local utility company to check for buried water mains, electrical cables, gas lines, etc. The inspector will flag the location of any buried utility lines with a marker similar to the one pictured here.

lines. These include water and sewer lines, as well as buried gas, electrical, and phone lines. After you've located the lines that service your own house, don't assume that more don't exist. In many housing tracts, utility companies have gained the right-of-way along front or back property lines for major underground power cables, water mains, cable TV service, or fiber-optic phone transmission lines. If you accidentally break a major phone line, TV cable, or water main while digging, you could be liable for thousands of dollars worth of damage. If you hit a major power line, the consequences could be fatal.

Utility companies often will locate underground utilities free of charge. Underground utilities servicing your house (water, gas, sewer, and electric) may be indicated on the original deed map or site plan for your property. If your home was built recently, the local building department may have a record of utility hookup locations on your property. If your home is older, additional lines may have been added in previous remodels or landscaping jobs.

If you are uncertain where such lines exist within your property, hire a private wire/pipe/cable locating firm. These firms are listed in the yellow pages of your phone book under the heading "Utilities Underground Cable, Pipe, & Wire Locating Service" or similar heading. They usually charge by the hour; a good firm can trace and mark all underground utilities on an average-size residential lot within one or two hours.

Avoiding Frost Heave

In areas subject to harsh winters, wet, fine-grained soils undergo a condition called "frost heave," in which alternate freezing and thawing causes the soil to shift, often with damaging results to any structure built on it. In severe cases, frost heave will push fence posts up, weakening the fence structure. Check with your local building department to determine frost depth and whether frost heave is a problem.

Where frost heave is a problem, fence posts must be set in holes with a gravel subbase that extends below the frost line. The frost line is the area below which frost doesn't penetrate in a typical winter. In areas where the frost line extends below 36 inches, consult your local building department for commonly accepted excavation practices that may save you from digging too deep.

Even in areas where frost heave is not a problem, good drainage is required around fences to avoid damage to these structures. Moisture magnifies ground movement and creates erosion that will make fences sink, lean, or crack; poor drainage around wood fence posts can lead to rotting. Gravel and sand are used to provide good drainage.

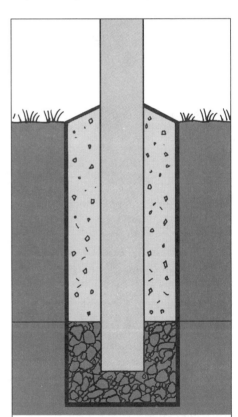

Avoiding Frost Heave. In areas subject to frost heave, dig postholes below the frost line, fill the first 4 to 6 inches with crushed stone, set the post, add more stone, and then pour a concrete collar. Slope the top.

SETTING POSTS

The first step in building a fence is marking the fence location with stakes and string. Once you've done that, mark post locations along the string with tape or bright-colored chalk. If you're installing the fence on a property line or if the fence must meet certain setback requirements, you'll need to establish the exact location of the line to avoid disputes with neighbors or to make sure the fence meets local ordinances. Once you've located your property lines, mark the corners with surveyor's stakes or other markers.

Plotting a Fence

Whether you're building a fence to define your property lines or you're installing one within the property, first you'll need to establish the locations of end posts and corner posts. Usually, this is done by measuring out from one or more existing reference points on the property, such as the house, the driveway, an existing fence, or other landmarks. If you haven't already done so, draw up a site plan and use the plan as a guide.

This section explains how to locate posts for a straight fence built on flat ground with corners meeting at 90 degrees. It is likely your situation is not so ideal, but with these instructions and a little common sense, you can lay out posts for just about any fence design.

1 **Marking the End Posts.** Drive a 1x2 stake firmly into the ground, marking each end of the fence line. Drive a small nail into the top of each stake marking what will be the center of the fence posts. Stakes typically project 4 to 6 inches above ground; however, taller stakes may be required for the twine to clear low obstructions along the fence line.

Digging the postholes will obliterate all your layout marks. Erect batter boards to make it easy to reestablish them. To build batter boards, drive two stakes about a foot apart, a few feet beyond each corner stake. Connect them with a crosspiece. Stretch mason's twine from crosspiece to crosspiece, positioning it so that it hits the nail on the corner stakes. (Use mason's twine because it does not sag as much as ordinary string.)

2 **Establishing a 90-degree corner.** If the fence will enclose a square or rectangular area, you'll want the corners to form an exact 90-degree angle. Lay out the corner using the 3-4-5 (or 6-8-10) triangle method. Begin with the side you have laid out, which has the corners A and B in the drawing. Put a batter board about 12 inches beyond the approximate location of the third corner and another one about 12 inches beyond the opposite corner—corner B in the drawing. String a line from crosspiece to crosspiece so that it hits the nail in the corner stake at point B. From the same corner stake, measure out 3 (or 6) feet along one string and 4 (or 8) feet along the other, and mark these measurements on the strings. Have a helper slide the string

along the far batter board until the diagonal distance between the marks equals 5 (or 10) feet. Mark the string location on the batter board. Mark the location of the end post on the string, hang a plumb bob or use a level to transfer this point to the ground, and drive a stake at this point (C) to mark the end of the fence.

3 **Establishing Additional Corners.** To enclose three sides of the property, run a second string out from a batter board at point A, attach it to another batter board, and repeat the above procedure. To form a complete enclosure (fenced on all four sides), drive two batter boards slightly beyond each of the corner locations, adjust the strings until they intersect at 90 degrees at all four corners, then drive stakes where strings intersect each other.

4 **Locating the Posts.** Once you've established the fence line with stakes and string, measure the total length of each side from corner to corner. Then, measure and mark post locations along the string, either by dividing the total length into equal intervals (do not exceed 96 inches between posts) or to make

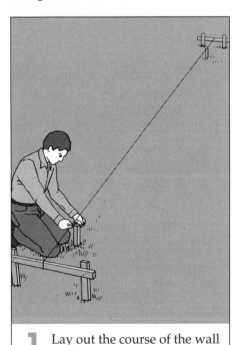

1 Lay out the course of the wall with mason's twine stretched between batter boards.

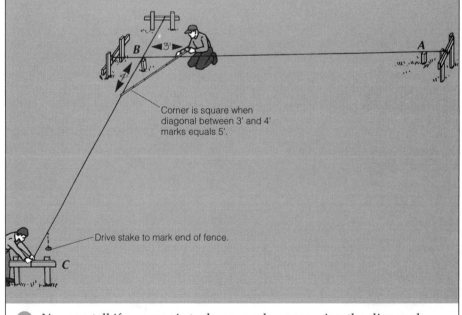

Corner is square when diagonal between 3' and 4' marks equals 5'.

Drive stake to mark end of fence.

2 You can tell if a corner is truly square by measuring the diagonal between a 3-foot and a 4-foot leg (or 6-ft. and 8-ft. leg). The corner is square if the diagonal measures 5 (or 10) feet.

best use of precut lumber lengths (48-, 72-, or 96-inch rails). Apply small pieces of tape to the string that mark the center of each post.

Unless you divide the overall length into equal sections, you will probably end up with a short section at one end. For example, if the total length of the fence line is 34 feet, you can either divide it into six equal sections measuring 68 inches, or you can divide the fence into five 72-inch sections, with a short 48-inch section at one end. If the fence includes a gate, you can place the short section at the gate location and build the gate to fit in the short section.

If you are using precut lumber for rails that will fit snugly between the posts, remember that the mark on the string indicates the center of the post, not the edge. Be sure to allow for the thickness of the post when doing your layout work. If you're using prefabricated fence panels, locate post centers so that the panels either fit snugly between them or butt together on the centerline of the posts. The method you choose depends on the particular panel design; consult manufacturer's instructions.

5 **Transferring Post Locations to the Ground.** Use a plumb bob to transfer the marks from the string to the ground, as shown. Mark each post location on the ground with a nail stuck through a piece of paper or with a stake. Once all of the marks are in place, remove the string.

Fences on a Slope

You have two basic design choices for hillside fencing: contoured fencing and stepped fencing. On a contoured fence, the rails run parallel with the slope, so the fence follows the contour of the ground. These fences are easier to construct than stepped fences, especially on the uneven slopes or rolling terrain that is typical of rural landscapes. Board fences, discussed on page 30, are another popular choice.

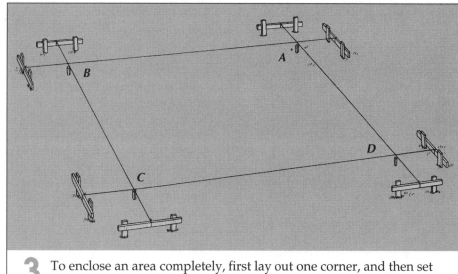

3 To enclose an area completely, first lay out one corner, and then set up batter boards and strings to lay out additional corners

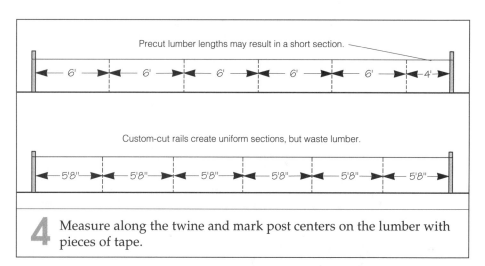

Precut lumber lengths may result in a short section.

6' → 6' → 6' → 6' → 6' → 4'

Custom-cut rails create uniform sections, but waste lumber.

5'8" → 5'8" → 5'8" → 5'8" → 5'8" → 5'8"

4 Measure along the twine and mark post centers on the lumber with pieces of tape.

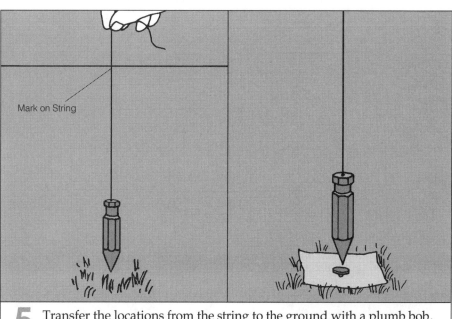

Mark on String

5 Transfer the locations from the string to the ground with a plumb bob, and mark each location with a nail, stuck through a piece of paper.

In some instances, you may find large barriers or obstacles, such as trees, boulders, or drainage areas, interfering with your chosen fence line. In such cases, you can remove the obstacle, move the fence line, or build the fence to skirt or incorporate the obstacle. The drawings show four common solutions for dealing with these obstacles.

If a tree stands in your fence line and you've decided to incorporate the tree into the fence, you should set the posts several feet away from the tree to avoid damaging its roots. Install the fence rails and then the siding so that they extend beyond the posts toward the tree. To keep these sections from sagging, install diagonal braces made from siding material, as shown. Cut the nearest boards to match the trunk profile. You can do this by placing the last board or boards against the tree and scribing a line with a compass to follow the trunk profile. Leave about 2 inches between the board and trunk to allow for tree growth. Cut along the marked line with a saber saw, then attach the board(s) to the rails. You can use the same technique to incorporate a boulder into the fence.

Where a fence crosses a low area, extend boards below the bottom rail to follow the contour, as shown.

Do not extend boards farther than about 8 inches below the bottom rail or the ends will tend to warp.

If the fence must cross a swale, ditch, or small stream that contains water during the rainy season, construct a grate from lengths of No. 3 rebar or 1/2-inch galvanized pipe, spaced about 6 inches apart, to keep people and large animals from crawling underneath the fence. Drill holes through a rail made from two 2x4s. Attach the rail to the fence, insert the pipe or rebar through the holes, and drive it firmly into the ground. For extra measure and safety, you may choose to set the grate into a ribbon of concrete.

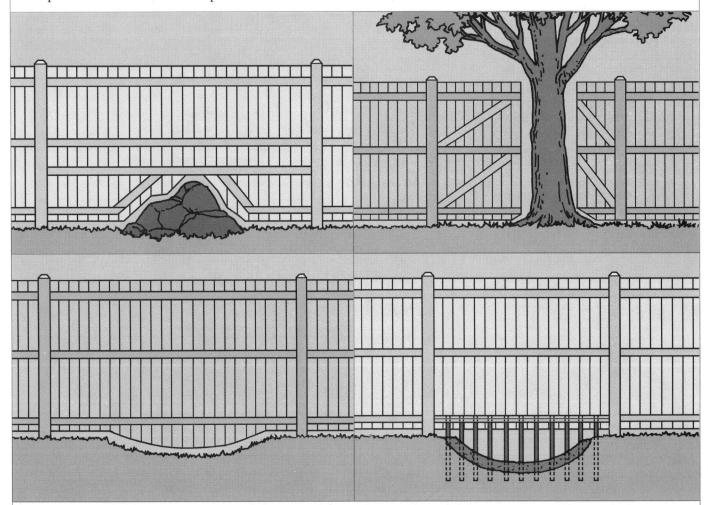

Dealing with Obstacles. Trees and boulders can be incorporated into the fence by setting the posts a few feet from the obstacle and extending the rails and siding from the posts. Cut the siding to match the profile of the obstacle, leaving a few inches of space. Extend siding below the bottom rail to cover low spots.

As the name implies, each section of a stepped fence steps up the hill like a stairway, usually in equal intervals. The top rail of each section is placed level; the bottom rail may be placed level or, more rarely, parallel with the slope. Stepped fences work best when the slope is fairly straight and even from top to bottom, so they're generally preferable in urban or suburban settings where the topography has been smoothed by grading and other landscaping. Also, the geometry of stepped fences reflects the strong horizontal and vertical lines of surrounding houses and other buildings.

Practically any fence design can be adapted to stepped fencing. On some solid-board or panel designs, however, the space beneath the bottom rails must be covered by extending the boards or panels below the rail to ground level. Such designs aren't recommended for steep slopes; if the boards extend more than about 8 inches below the bottom rail, they're likely to warp.

Plotting a Contoured Fence

This type of fence is laid out similarly to a straight fence along level ground. The only difference is that you may need extra stakes to keep a very hilly landscape from interfering with the layout lines.

1 **Plotting Fence Line.** Drive a stake at each end-post location and run mason's twine between the stakes. Make sure the stakes are tall enough so that the twine clears any obstructions or minor changes in terrain. If the terrain is very uneven, you may need to install intermediate stakes to keep the twine from touching the ground.

2 **Locating the Posts.** Measure along the line and mark intermediate post locations with chalk or small pieces of tape. Then use a plumb bob to transfer post locations to the ground, and mark these spots with stakes or nails stuck through paper scraps (see "Transferring Post Locations to the Ground," page 13).

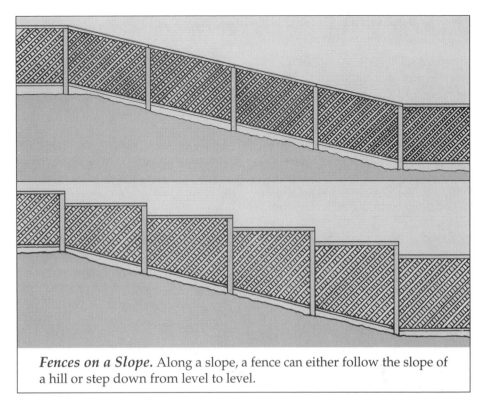

Fences on a Slope. Along a slope, a fence can either follow the slope of a hill or step down from level to level.

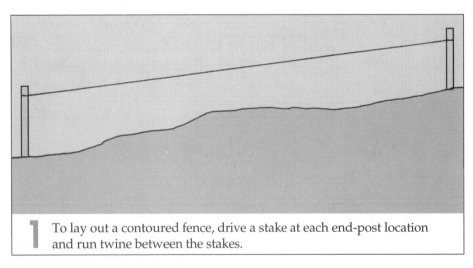

1 To lay out a contoured fence, drive a stake at each end-post location and run twine between the stakes.

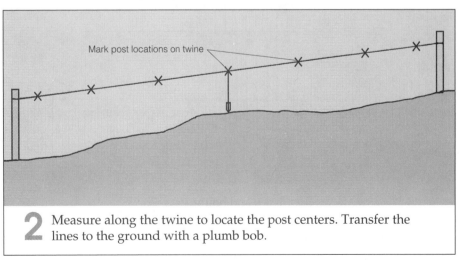

Mark post locations on twine

2 Measure along the twine to locate the post centers. Transfer the lines to the ground with a plumb bob.

Once all the marks are in place, remove the string.

When installing posts for contoured fencing, set each post to exactly the same height above the ground (72 inches, for example). Fasten the rails at the same height along the posts, so they follow the contour of the slope. (The top rails might meet the posts at 70 inches above the ground. The bottom rails meet the posts at 6 inches above the ground.) Install fence boards so that they are plumb, rather than perpendicular to the slope of the rails. Extend the boards several inches below the bottom rail, and cut the ends to follow the contour of the ground.

Plotting a Stepped Fence

A stepped fence is more difficult to plot than a contoured fence because you must work from a level reference line. Having a level line to work from is an efficient way to locate posts for a fence with level rails. If the slope is very steep or the fence run is very long, you may want to hire a fence contractor to plot the fence for you. For gradual slopes or shorter sections of fence, proceed as follows:

1 **Establishing a Level Line.** Drive a short stake marking the post location at the top of the hill and a tall stake marking the location at the bottom of the hill. The lower stake must be tall enough so that you can stretch a level line between the two stakes. The lower stake must also be plumb, so check it with a level to be sure it is standing straight up and down. Attach mason's twine to the stakes and use a line level to level the twine.

2 **Marking the Post Locations.** Measure along the leveled string and mark post locations with chalk or pieces of tape. As mentioned earlier, you can space the posts evenly by dividing the fence into equal sections, but to make the best use of precut lumber sizes, consider spac-

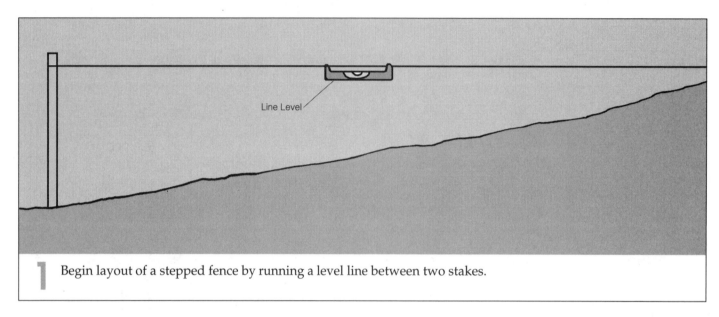

1 Begin layout of a stepped fence by running a level line between two stakes.

Line Level

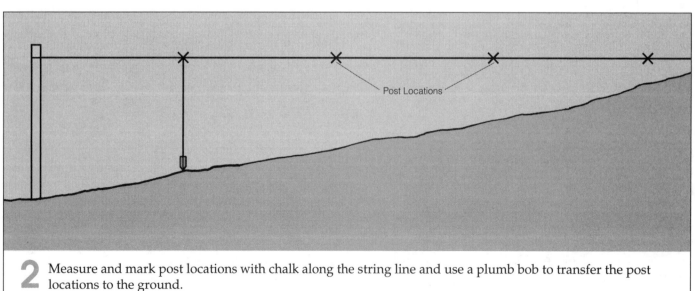

2 Measure and mark post locations with chalk along the string line and use a plumb bob to transfer the post locations to the ground.

Post Locations

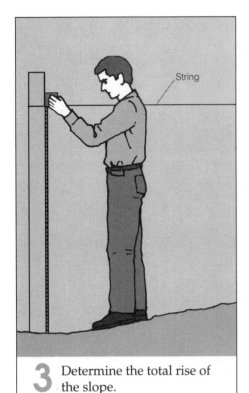

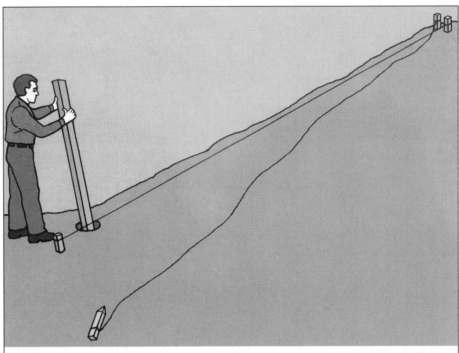

3 Determine the total rise of the slope.

4 Run a string between two stakes to locate the front of the post. Dig each hole and install each post starting from the bottom of the slope.

ing the posts 72 to 96 inches apart. Transfer the post locations to the ground with a plumb bob, then mark them with stakes or pieces of paper stuck with nails.

3 Determining the Step Size. The most attractive stepped fences have the same step height between sections. To figure out the step height, first you must determine the overall height of the slope. Measure the distance from the ground to the string at the lower end post. This measurement is the overall height or rise of the slope. Divide the rise by the number of sections (the areas between the posts) to determine the size of the step. For example, if the total rise is 48 inches, and the fence contains four equal sections, there should be 12-inch steps between posts.

4 Setting the First Post. Before you dig intermediate holes, string a line between your layout stakes so the posts form a neat line stepping up the slope. Begin digging at the bottom of the hill. Dig the hole and insert the post, as described in "Installing Posts" on page 18. The height of this

5 Mark the step height on each post.

post depends on the fence style. With some fence styles, the posts are as high as the siding. With other styles, the siding projects above the posts. In this example, the top rail will be fastened across the top of the post, and the siding can either project above the rail or be installed level with it.

5 Marking the Step Heights. Before setting the rest of the posts, mark the step heights on the posts. From the top of each post, measure the distance of the step height (12 inches in this example) and mark the point with a pencil and a square.

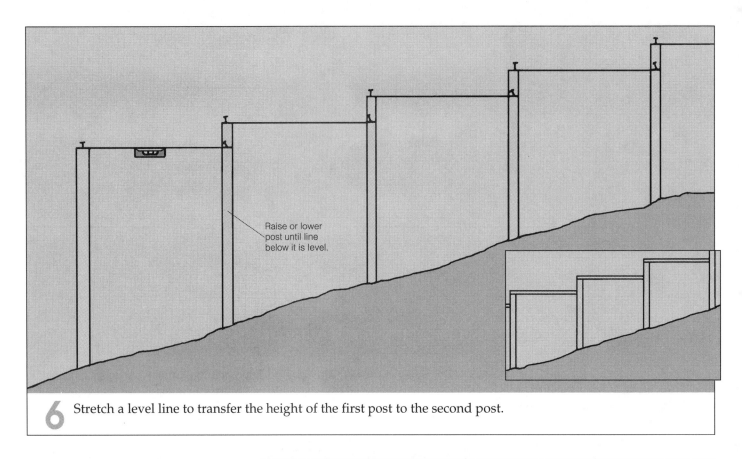

6 Stretch a level line to transfer the height of the first post to the second post.

Raise or lower post until line below it is level.

6 Setting the Line Posts. Set the successive uphill posts (the line posts, as opposed to the end posts) so that the step-height marks you penciled on them are level with tops of the previous posts. Use a line level or a level and a long, straight board to set the posts to the correct height.

7 Setting the End Post. If the fence levels off and continues at the top of the hill, set the top post as you did the other posts. If the fence ends at the top of the hill, set the post temporarily and mark a cut-off line that is level with the previous post. Remove the end post, cut it, and set it permanently as described below.

Installing Posts

As a rule of thumb, fence posts are set with at least one-third of their total length in the ground, at a minimum of 24 inches deep. In areas subject to frost heave, it is recommended that you set the bottoms of the posts at least 6 inches below the frost line. But you always should check local codes and standard practices in your particular area. The one-third rule applies especially to gate, end, and corner posts, and ones that support heavy siding materials. Solid-board or panel fences subject to high winds may also require deeper posts. However, the rule doesn't always make best use of standard precut lumber lengths (a 72-inch fence would

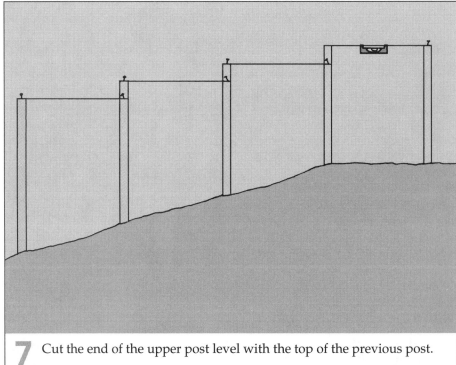

7 Cut the end of the upper post level with the top of the previous post.

require a 9-foot post, for example). For this reason, most 72-inch fences can use 96-inch posts sunk 24 inches in the ground. The end posts, corner posts, and gate posts on such a fence should still be the full 9 feet long.

1 **Digging the Postholes.** Use a posthole digger to dig post-holes 4 to 6 inches deeper than the intended post depth. The extra depth will be backfilled with gravel or rubble to facilitate drainage beneath the post. The gravel also prevents concrete (if used) from sealing off the post bottom, trapping water beneath the post and making it susceptible to freezing.

Keep the holes as narrow as possible; usually about twice the width of the post. In boggy soils or heavy clay soils subject to frost heave, you may need to dig wider holes, and backfill with compacted sand and gravel or gravel and concrete. (To help you decide which backfill material to use, see "Choosing Backfill Materials," page 22.) If you're adding a stabilizing concrete collar in very loose or sandy soil, make the hole diameter about three times the width of the post (12 inches for a 4-inch post). Dig all of the postholes before you start setting the posts. To dig all holes to the same depth, measure from the end of the tool's digger blade to a point on the handle equal to the desired hole depth and mark with a felt-tip pen.

2 **Setting the First Post.** Relocate the layout twine to mark the face of the posts instead of the center. If you used batter boards, simply move the twine sideways half the thickness of the posts. If you used stakes, drive new stakes that are centered roughly half the post thickness away from the original layout line. Drive nails in the stakes marking the faces of the posts, and run twine between them.

No matter what type of backfill you're using—earth, gravel, or concrete—start by shoveling 5 to 6 inches of coarse gravel into the hole and tamping it firmly.

Set the post in the hole and check the height. Add gravel to adjust the height. Then hold the post gently

against the layout twine, while a helper shovels in about 4 to 6 inches of gravel.

Hold a 24-inch level on adjacent faces and move the post into plumb while a helper backfills the hole.

3 **Tamping the Earth and Gravel Fill.** Add the backfill several inches at a time, tamping vigorously with a length of 2x4 as you go. Periodically check that the post is plumb.

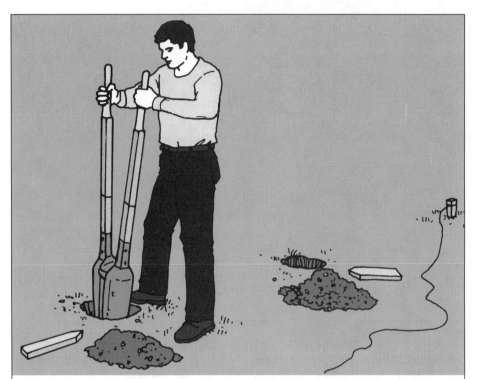

1 Dig postholes 4-6 inches deeper than the bottom of the post so that you can put gravel in the hole for drainage. The hole should be three times as wide as the post, if you're using a concrete collar.

2 Stretch a line between stakes or batter boards to position the faces of the posts.

3 If you choose to backfill the hole with dirt, tamp it with a 2x4, and check the post for plumb while you work.

4 Backfilling with Concrete. To save time and effort, some do-it-yourselfers use the posthole as a wheelbarrow and mix everything in the ground. This works in very dense soil that is more like rock than dirt. But in most situations, it folds dirt and debris into the concrete, alters the mix proportions, and weakens the post. You'd get better results eliminating the concrete altogether and setting the post in dirt that is backfilled and tamped down in stages. If you're using concrete, the best mixing method has two operations. First, stir all dry ingredients in a wheelbarrow or other clean container to make sure cement, sand, and aggregate are evenly distributed (even if the mix comes from a bag). Second, add water and stir again until the entire batch is equally moist. After you shovel the mix into the hole, plunge a length of reinforcing rod (or your shovel handle) into the wet concrete several times to remove air pockets.

5 Temporarily Bracing the Post. Slope the top of the concrete collar to help shed water. Be careful not to knock the post out of alignment while the concrete is setting up. Then set up temporary 2x4 braces nailed

4 You can mix some types of concrete right in the hole, but it's better to premix. Moisten the surrounding area, and then pour in the mixed ingredients. Plunge the shovel handle in the hole to remove air pockets.

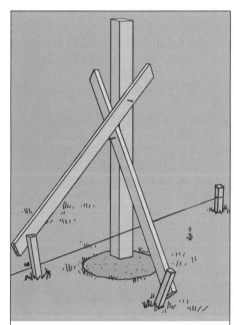

5 Brace the post to hold it plumb while the concrete sets and dries.

with duplex nails to the post and to stakes in the ground to keep the post plumb. Leave the braces in place until the concrete has cured sufficiently (about 2 hours with a fast-setting mix, or 24 to 48 hours with a conventional mix). It's best to set and brace all the fence posts, and install the rails and siding after the concrete has cured.

6 Setting the Other End Post. Measure the height of the first post, and set the other end post to the same height, making sure it is plumb as you add the backfill. To keep the posts aligned, run mason's twine from the face of one end post to the other. Tack the twine in place so that it is 6 inches from the tops of the posts.

7 Setting the Line Posts. Just as you set the corner or end posts, set the intermediate or line posts. Position the posts so they just touch the strings. Measure from the upper length of string to the top of the posts to keep the line posts at the same height as the end posts. Check the posts with a level as you work.

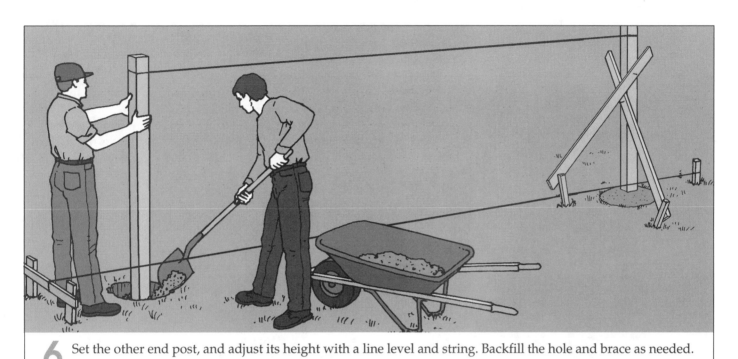

6 Set the other end post, and adjust its height with a line level and string. Backfill the hole and brace as needed.

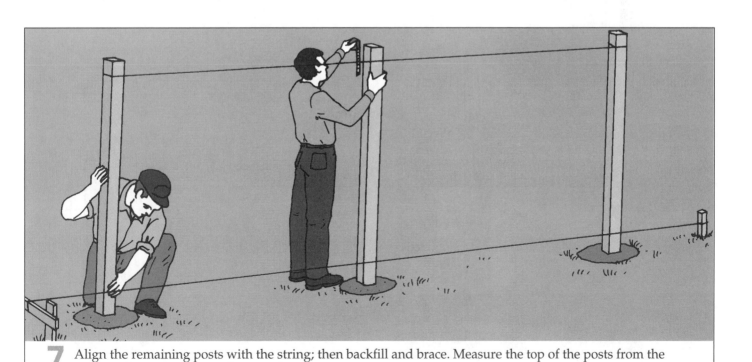

7 Align the remaining posts with the string; then backfill and brace. Measure the top of the posts from the string to keep the posts at the same height.

Typically, posts are set in tamped earth, earth and gravel, or concrete and gravel. Whether or not you decide to use concrete depends largely on the fence design and soil conditions. Generally, you can use earth-and-gravel fill if the soil is not too loose, sandy, subject to shifting or frost heaves, and if the fence posts don't have to support much weight. Post and board fences, lattice, spaced pickets, or fences under 60 inches tall are all light enough for earth-and-gravel fill. In extremely loose or sandy soils, you can attach 1x4 pressure-treated cleats to the bottoms of the posts with nails, as shown, to provide lateral stability. A base stone is not required in this procedure.

For added stability, use concrete, especially in areas with deep frost lines. You can even drive 16d nails partially into the post before placing the concrete to lock the post and concrete together. If precise post spacing is required (such as when dadoing or mortising rails into posts, or attaching prefabricated fence panels or sections), you'll need to set the posts successively, fitting in rails or sections as you set each post. Fast-setting concrete mixes are preferred for this type of construction. After pouring the concrete and attaching the first set of rails or panel, install temporary braces at post locations to keep the fence section plumb while the concrete sets. As you fill in successive sections, occasionally recheck the entire fence for plumb, and adjust the temporary braces if necessary.

If you're unsure of local building practices, seek advice from the building department or ask several local fence contractors for recommended practices in your area.

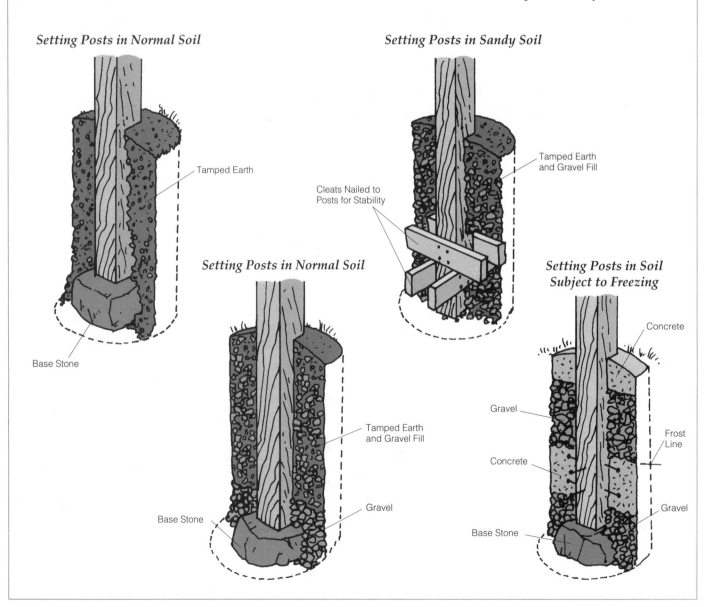

Setting Posts in Normal Soil

Tamped Earth

Base Stone

Setting Posts in Sandy Soil

Tamped Earth and Gravel Fill

Cleats Nailed to Posts for Stability

Setting Posts in Normal Soil

Tamped Earth and Gravel Fill

Base Stone

Gravel

Setting Posts in Soil Subject to Freezing

Concrete

Gravel

Concrete

Frost Line

Base Stone

Gravel

BUILDING THE FENCE

Rails and siding give a fence both its character and strength. Rails are the horizontal parts of the fence frame. The siding includes things like pickets, boards, or paneling, and is usually supported by the rails. Many localities have strict rules that apply to fences. Before you begin to build, check with the local building department to see whether your wood fence meets ordinances and restrictions regarding setbacks, height, and structural requirements.

Board Fences

In most cases, the basic framework for wood fences consists of 4x4 posts and 2x4 rails to which you attach boards or panels. Make sure you use wood suitable for outdoor use. The least-expensive solution depends in part on where you live. The most durable timber is pressure-treated lumber. In the Northwest, however, redwood and cedar may be significantly cheaper than pressure-treated wood and could be more cost effective. Elsewhere, however, it's a good idea to use pressure-treated wood at least for the posts, if not the rest of the fence. If your budget allows, you can still use redwood or cedar for the more visible parts of the fence, such as caps, rails, and siding. Avoid untreated pine or Douglas fir. They don't hold up well, even when painted.

Prefab Fences

If you want to avoid the design process and save a considerable amount of time and effort building a fence, consider buying prefabricated fence panels. Made of wood, metal, or PVC plastic, the panels come preassembled in 36-, 48-, 72-, and 96-inch sections, in heights from 36 to 96 inches. Some designs also come with matching gates and other features, such as prefabricated arbors. Most lumberyards and home centers stock a few popular designs. You can order others through catalogs or brochures available at the service desk.

To build a prefab board fence, set the posts at the proper spacing, depending on the length of the panels, and fasten the panels to the posts. Installation techniques vary among manufacturers, but most panels with horizontal rails and vertical siding are fastened to the posts with fence brackets. Complete installation instructions are provided by the manufacturer.

Most stores sell a variety of prefab picket fence panels, as well as several other popular styles. Prefab wood panels are the closest thing to an instant fence. The panels don't cost much more than if you had bought everything separately and built the fence from scratch. Quality of materials and factory assembly are sometimes mediocre. Check the panels carefully for defects in materials and workmanship, and make sure they're sturdy enough to meet your needs.

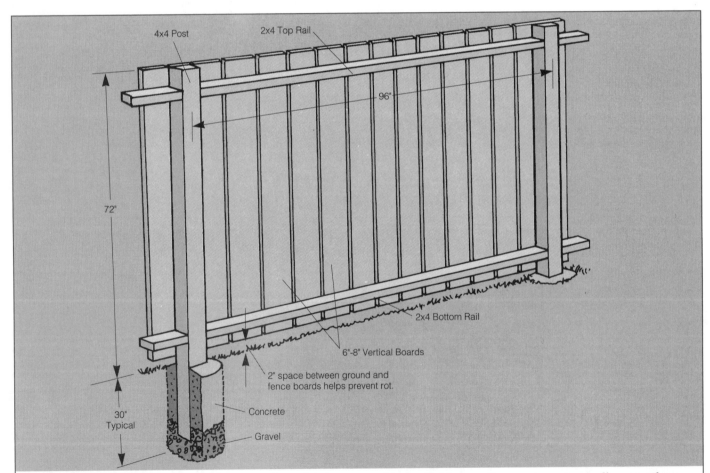

Board Fences. A typical board fence consists of 4x4 posts and 2x4 rails. Supporting posts are typically spaced on either 72- or 96-inch centers.

Sometimes, a sharp corner can evoke an objectionable, boxed-in feeling, or create a dangerous blind spot for drivers. Curves soften sharp angles in fences and are less likely to obstruct views. To build a curved fence, you must set the posts on 48- to 72-inch centers along an arc. You can apply either straight or curved rails, depending on the look you are trying to create. It takes curved rails to make a truly curved fence, but making curved rails is not as difficult as you might think. As shown in the drawing, each rail consists of two separate pieces of 1x4 redwood screwed together to form a laminated rail. The rails must span at least three posts—they won't form a curve if they span only two. Stagger the joints so that a joint on the top rail is not on the same post as a joint on the bottom rail.

In the design shown, the rails are let into 3½-inch wide by 1½-inch deep dadoes cut into the posts. Soak rails in water before use to make them more flexible. Attach the first piece to the posts with 3-inch galvanized deck screws, using two screws at each post. Then screw the second piece over the first, using 1¼-inch galvanized decking screws, spaced about 8 inches apart. Stagger the screws so that one is near the top of the rail, the other near the bottom.

For tighter arcs, you can laminate thinner redwood strips, called benderboards, or cut a series of ¼-inch deep saw cuts, called kerfs, about 2 inches apart in the one-by-fours to make them more flexible. Place the kerfed side against the posts. In all cases, the laminated rails should be a total of 1¼ to 1½ inches thick to support the weight of the siding.

True-curve fences look best with narrow, lightweight boards, slats, pickets, or rough-split redwood grapestakes attached vertically to the rails. Wide boards may split when attached to curved rails.

Segmented Fences. Instead of curved rails, you can attach short, straight fence sections to posts plotted along a curve. Technically, this type of construction does not result in a smooth curve. Instead, you get a series of short, straight chords that roughly follow an arc. On this type of fence, you miter the rail ends and the siding before fastening them to the face of the post, as shown. Drive the fasteners at the point where the rail touches the post for the strongest connection. Because the rails are straight, you can use wide boards or plywood for the siding.

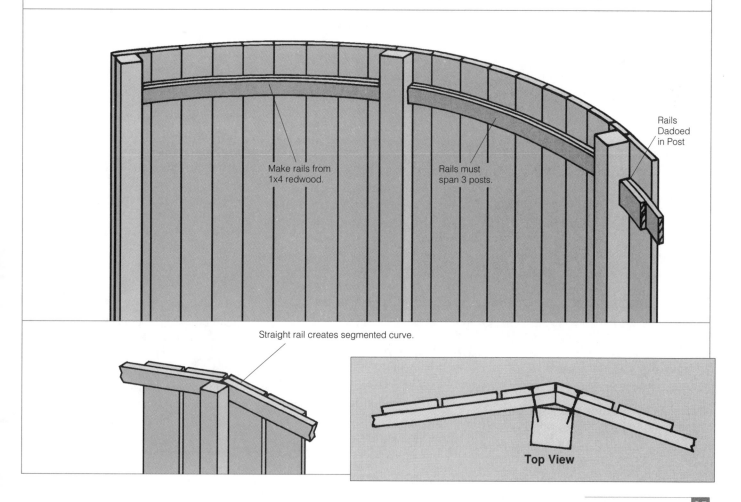

Make rails from 1x4 redwood.

Rails must span 3 posts.

Rails Dadoed in Post

Straight rail creates segmented curve.

Top View

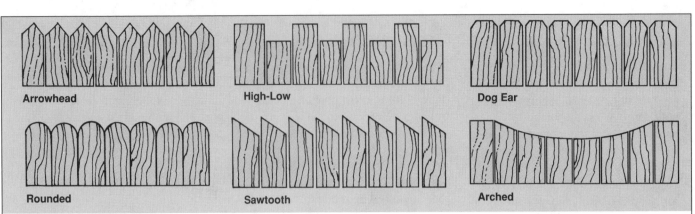

Board-Top Variations. You can add interest to vertical-board fences by changing the shape of the top. Except for the arched fence, all board tops are cut before you attach them to the fence. For an arched design, attach boards with tops flush, and cut them to shape later.

Board fences are the most common wood fence in urban and suburban yards. The design options for them are virtually limitless.

Most board fences use ¾-inch thick siding in widths ranging from 3 to 12 inches. Mid-size boards 6 or 8 inches wide are popular because they're usually most economical. They're also less likely to cup and split than wider ones.

You can also use house siding such as shiplap, clapboard, channel rustic, and others.

Typical Construction. Most board fences consist of siding boards nailed to one side of the frame, creating a board side and a frame side. In front or side yards, you typically place the board, or good, side toward the street because it looks better. On property-line fences, it is customary to face the good side toward your neighbor's yard to avoid ill feelings.

Some fences look the same on both sides. You might want to build one of these fences for marking property lines. Some of these good-neighbor designs include the "Vertical Board-on-Board Fence," page 33, "Alternating Panel Fence," page 34, and "Louver Fence," page 35.

Board-Top Variations. Many siding materials can be oriented horizontally, vertically, or diagonally to match the house style. On vertical-board designs, the board tops can be cut at angles to shed water, prolonging the life of the boards. Decorative cuts also add interest to the fence design, as does altering board width and direction. Using other types of wood or incorporating lattice, battens, or exterior moldings also adds visual appeal.

Property-Line Fences: Know Where to Draw the Line

You need to know the exact location of the property line before you build a fence to mark it. If your fence is just 1 inch on your neighbor's side of the line, you might have to tear down the fence or face a lawsuit. In many newer subdivisions, the original survey stakes (usually a marked metal rod or wood stake driven in the ground at each corner of the property) may still be in place. If they are, show them to your neighbors and have them agree in writing that these stakes represent the actual boundaries. If you can't locate the stakes or think they may have been moved from their original position, hire a surveyor to relocate and mark the property lines, and file a record of the survey with the county. Although a simple survey of a residential tract lot can cost a few hundred dollars, it is cheap insurance against future boundary disputes, especially if you're sinking thousands of dollars into your landscape project.

Most property fences are directly on the property line. No matter who builds the structure, you and your adjoining neighbors legally own it as tenants in common. This means that your neighbors can do what they want to their side of the fence—grow vines on it, paint murals—anything short of actually damaging or tearing down the structure.

The best course of action is to inform the neighbors of your plans and enlist their cooperation, if possible. Then, try to come up with a design that satisfies all parties involved. With traditional board fences, it's customary (though not legally required) to build the fence so that the board side, not the frame side, faces the neighbor's property. However, there are a variety of good-neighbor designs that look equally good from both sides. (See page 27 for examples.)

If you reach an impasse with any neighbor, simply build the fence 12 inches on your side of the property line. Then you can build anything you want without the neighbor's permission or cooperation, as long as the structure meets local codes and ordinances. Bear in mind that you'll be totally responsible for maintaining the fence.

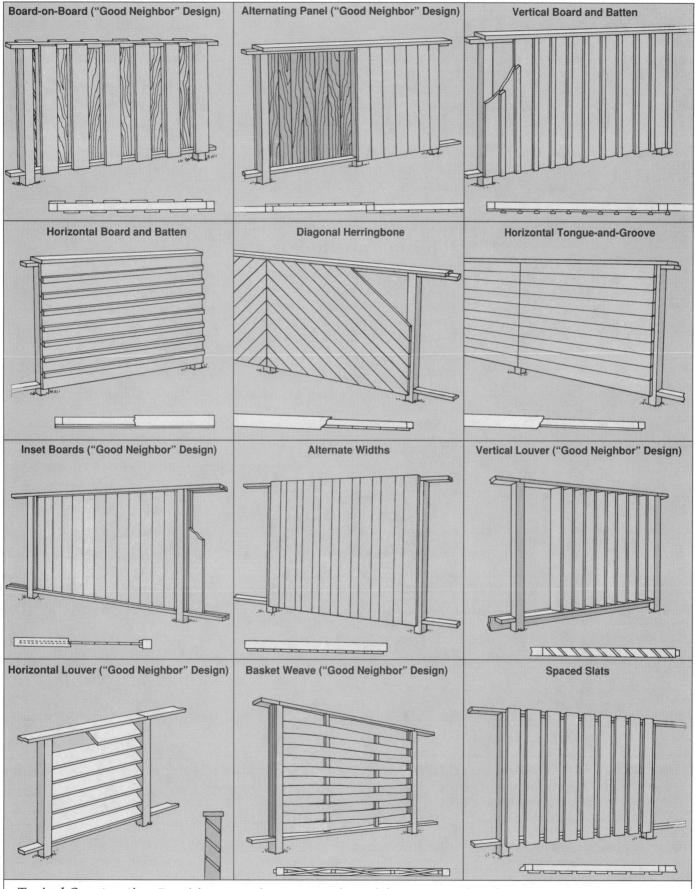

Board-on-Board ("Good Neighbor" Design)

Alternating Panel ("Good Neighbor" Design)

Vertical Board and Batten

Horizontal Board and Batten

Diagonal Herringbone

Horizontal Tongue-and-Groove

Inset Boards ("Good Neighbor" Design)

Alternate Widths

Vertical Louver ("Good Neighbor" Design)

Horizontal Louver ("Good Neighbor" Design)

Basket Weave ("Good Neighbor" Design)

Spaced Slats

Typical Construction. Board fences are the most popular and there are countless design variations.

Post and Rail Variations. Many board-fence designs incorporate a 1x6 or 2x6 cap rail nailed across the post tops to help protect the fence below. Angling the cap rail discourages young fence climbers from walking along the top of the fence. To angle the cap rail, cut the post tops at a 30-degree angle. Then set all the posts to the same height by adding or removing gravel below the post. But it's easier to set untrimmed,

long posts, strike a chalk line to mark the post tops, and cut the angle with the posts in place. Mark the angle on the first post, and then duplicate it by snapping a chalk line across other posts, and transferring the slope with a bevel square. Unlike a typical square, this type is hinged so you can set and lock any angle (the slope on the first post), and duplicate it on every other post in the fence. If you don't have this tool, cut the angle on a scrap piece of wood.

Joining Rails to Posts

Depending on your fence design, you can join the rails to the posts in a variety of ways. The following instructions are for joining 2x4 rails to 4x4 posts—the basic framework for many fences.

In most cases, top and bottom rails are simply butted between the posts. As a rule, the bottom rail is placed 2 to 8 inches above ground level and the top rail is placed 4 to 8 inches

below the post top. Add a center rail if you're building a fence with heavy siding materials, or if the rails span more than 72 inches. Mark where the rails meet the posts with a chalk line and line level. Cut the rails one by one to fit snugly between the posts. Attach with nails or screws. This type of construction depends entirely on the strength of the fasteners to support the sections of fencing, so consider using fence brackets or T-plates to beef up the connection between rails and posts. The connectors add strength but you may consider them unattractive.

In some fence designs, the top rails are fastened to the tops of the posts (see the drawings on page 27). For strength, top rails should span at least three posts. Butt the joints halfway across the post where they meet. Drill pilot holes in the top rail ends before fastening them with nails or screws. Where post rails butt together on a post, drive two 10d nails or two 3½-inch galvanized

A
Angled Post Top
Rail

B
Chamfered Post Top
Rail

C
Chamfered Cap Rail
Top Rail

D
Angled Top Rail

Post and Rail Variations. (A) An angled post top facilitates water runoff. (B) A chamfered post top helps water run off and gives the post a finished appearance. (C) A chamfered cap rail protects the structure beneath. (D) An angled cap rail discourages walking along the top of the fence.

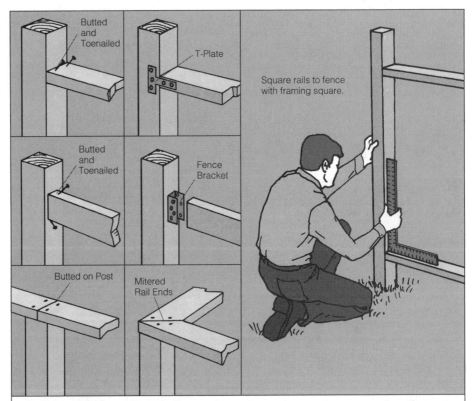

Butted and Toenailed
T-Plate
Butted and Toenailed
Fence Bracket
Butted on Post
Mitered Rail Ends
Square rails to fence with framing square.

Joining Rails to Posts. Shown here are various ways to attach rails to posts. Butt joints are the weakest; you can strengthen these joints with metal connectors. Always check to make sure rails are square with posts.

deck screws in each end of the rail. When the rail runs across a post, attach it with four fasteners.

Dadoing Posts. For increased strength and a more traditional appearance, cut notches in the posts to house the rails. Although you can cut these notches (called dadoes) after setting the posts, it is easier to cut them with the posts lying flat across two sawhorses. Mark the dado locations carefully, and be sure to set all of the posts to exactly the same height or the dadoes—and therefore the rails—won't be level.

To cut dadoes, measure from the top of the post, and mark the top and bottom of each dado with straight lines. Then make a series of ½-inch deep cuts between the lines with a hand saw or circular saw. Remove the waste with a hammer and chisel. Cut the bottom of each post to the exact length before setting it in the posthole.

Making the Connection. Although nails are easiest to use and least expensive to buy, many fence builders prefer screws for joining rails to posts (and sometimes boards to rails). That's because screws make a stronger connection. They are also more easily removed if you make a mistake or want to repair the fence later. No matter which fastener you choose, however, it's best to predrill holes to avoid splitting the rail ends. Make the holes about ⅔ the diameter of your nails or screws.

If your fence is not dadoed and you're not attaching the rails with fence hardware, simply butt the rails between the posts. To attach them, toenail 10d galvanized nails or similar-sized screws through the top and bottom edges of the rail. Start by placing the rail flat on the ground. Start a screw or nail about 1½ inches from the end of the rail and drive it at an angle. Have a helper hold the opposite end of the board level while you nail one end to the first post at the mark you made. Then nail the opposite end.

Installing Kickboards. To prevent decay and termite infestation, keep

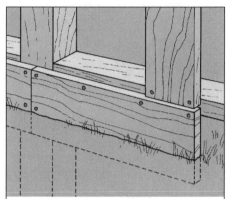

Installing Kickboards. A kickboard strengthens the fence and prevents animals from crawling under the structure.

For the strongest possible connection, dado the rail into the post.

Begin the dado by making a series of cuts into the post.

Knock out the waste with a chisel to finish the dado.

Dadoing Posts. First make a series of shallow cuts into the post, then knock out the waste. Dadoes can be cut before or after setting posts.

Preventing Sagging Rails

With time, many fences begin to droop or sag, especially toward the middle of a section that spans more than 72 inches. Placing the rails on edge, rather than flat, will help prevent sagging. Another way you can prevent sagging rails is to nail or screw a 2x4 vertical support midway between posts. First, cut a support long enough to fit under the top rail and extend about 24 inches into the ground. Then cut half-lap notches in the bottom rail and in the support, as shown, so that the outside edge of the support is flush with the outside edge of the rail. Set the support in concrete and gravel, as you would a fence post.

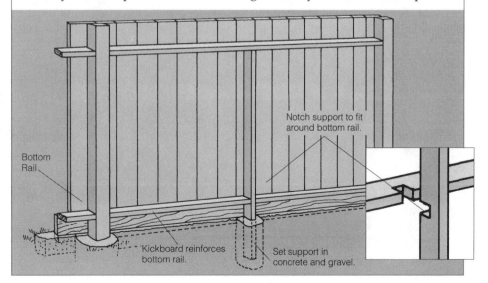

Bottom Rail

Notch support to fit around bottom rail.

Kickboard reinforces bottom rail.

Set support in concrete and gravel.

the bottom ends of the siding at least 2 inches above the ground. If you don't want a gap under the fence, you can attach a horizontal 1x8 or 1x10 kickboard along the bottoms of the posts. Notch the kickboard to fit around major obstructions, if necessary. The kickboard adds strength to the fence and is one way of correcting a fence sag. Attach the kickboard before you attach the siding, and make sure you leave enough room for a gap between the two. Allow a ¼- to ½-inch gap between the bottoms of the pickets and the top edge of the kickboard to help prevent decay.

Although you can simply set the kickboard on the ground, burying the bottom edge several inches below ground level will block water runoff and discourage animals from digging underneath. Make sure the kickboard material is designated for below-grade use.

Popular Board Fences

The following projects show how to add a variety of siding materials (boards, pickets, and plywood) to the post-and-rail frame, and in several cases, how to modify the frame to accept the siding. Also included are projects for simple post-and-rail and post-and-board fences, in which the rails also serve as the siding. All of these designs can be modified to suit your particular requirements.

Installing a Solid-Board Privacy Fence

Solid-board privacy fences are easy to build and go well with practically any style house. The most common solid-board fences are 72 inches high and use 1x6, 1x8, or 1x10 siding. Board tops can be cut in a variety of patterns (see "Board-Top Variations" on page 26). A dog-ear fence is shown here.

1 **Building the Frame.** Set the posts and attach the rails. This design calls for a center rail installed halfway between the top and bottom rails to keep the boards from warping.

2 **Cutting the Board Tops.** This step is optional. You might choose to make decorative cuts on the board tops for appearance or to shed water. To speed cutting, clamp several boards together with the top board marked for cutting, and cut three or more boards at a time with a hand saw, saber saw, portable circular saw, or power miter saw. Save one top board as a template for marking and cutting additional boards to the same shape.

3 **Attaching the Boards.** Start by attaching strings to the end posts about 2 inches above the ground on the face of the posts that will hold the siding. Level the string with a string level, and align

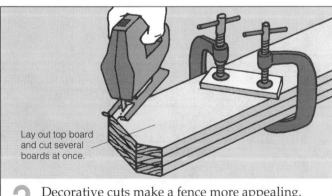

Installing a Solid-Board Privacy Fence. This fence has a board side and a frame side. The vertical boards butted together provide privacy.

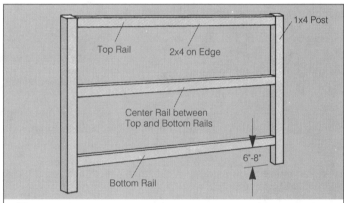

1 Set the posts and attach the rails, making sure the rails are square with the posts. A center rail is installed to prevent the boards from warping.

Lay out top board and cut several boards at once.

2 Decorative cuts make a fence more appealing. Save time by cutting several boards at once.

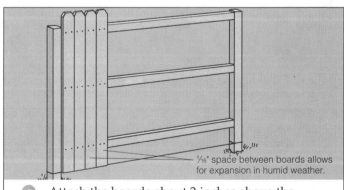

¹⁄₁₆" space between boards allows for expansion in humid weather.

3 Attach the boards about 2 inches above the ground. Use a string level as a guide.

the bottoms of the boards with it as you install them. If you want to conceal the post, begin by holding the board flush with the outside edge. If you don't want to conceal the post, hold the board flush with the inside edge of the end post, as shown. Then attach the board to the frame. For boards up to 6 inches wide, drill two pilot holes for either 8d galvanized nails or 2-inch galvanized deck screws. For wider boards, drill pilots for three nails or screws. Leave a 1/16-inch gap between boards as you install them to allow for expansion in humid or wet weather. (Use 4d nails as spacers.)

4 Attaching the Corner Boards. Where two fence runs meet at a corner, overlap the end boards, as shown, to hide the post. This often requires ripping one or both siding boards to a narrower width so that they fit. Rip boards on a table saw or with a portable circular saw equipped with an edge guide. For outside corners, attach the corner boards to the posts with 8d galvanized nails or 2-inch deck screws, spaced about 18 inches apart and 2 inches in from the corner. For a more finished appearance, you can cover the exposed board edge with 1x3 battens or trim.

For inside corners, simply overlap the boards. Attach them to the rails as you did the other boards. The joint formed by the lapped boards can be covered with a 1x1 or 2x2 strip or other molding. If desired, finish the corner with a mitered cap rail (see "Joining Rails to Posts," page 28).

Building a Horizontal-Board Fence

This solid horizontal-board fence has a formal appearance that's well-suited to contemporary home designs. The fence shown uses 96-inch 1x6s attached horizontally between posts on 96-inch centers. In this design, all posts should be exactly the same height. This design does not work well on sloped or uneven terrain. Attach 2x4 nailers

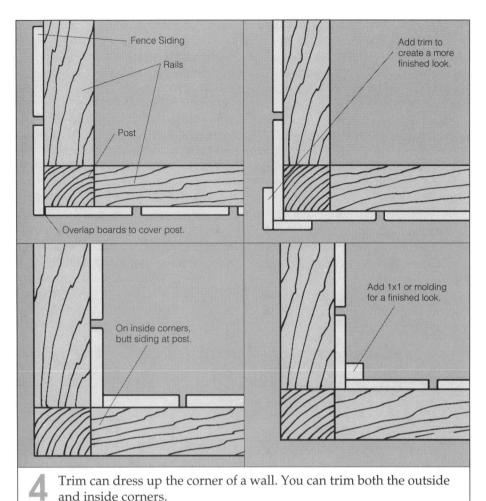

4 Trim can dress up the corner of a wall. You can trim both the outside and inside corners.

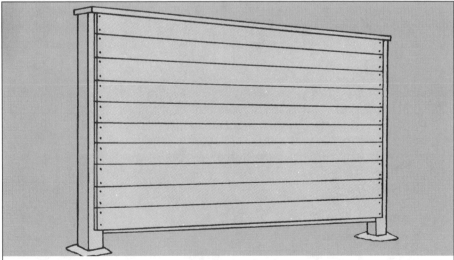

Building a Horizontal-Board Fence. This fence's long horizontal lines go well with contemporary house designs. The siding can consist of boards or wood to match your house.

midway between posts to provide additional nailing surface for the boards. A 2x4 vertical center support keeps the boards from bowing and the bottom rail from sagging. Drop siding, V-groove siding, shiplap, and other conventional house siding materials work well to make a fence that complements the wood siding on your house.

1 **Attaching the Cap Rail and Bottom Rails.** Install the 1x6 cap rail across the tops of the posts. Position the cap to overhang the front and back of the posts by 1 inch. Attach 2x4 bottom rails to the posts so they are level and at least 2 inches above ground level.

2 **Attaching the Center Support.** Cut the 2x4 center supports to fit between the rail and cap. Fasten the supports midway between the posts. The support should be flush with the face of the bottom rail, but recessed 1 inch from the front edge of the cap rail. Drive two galvanized 16d nails or 3½-inch deck screws through the cap rail into the support. Toenail the support to the bottom rail with 10d

nails or 2-inch galvanized deck screws. Put a block under the bottom rail to hold it steady when toenailing the center support.

3 **Attaching the Boards.** Cut the siding boards to span at least two posts. All ends should fall at the middle of a post face. Starting at the top, position the first board tightly under the cap-rail overhang. Attach the boards with two galvanized 8d ring-shank nails at the posts and the vertical support. Install the remaining boards, leaving 1/16 inch between the boards to allow for expansion in wet weather. You might have to rip the bottom board flush with the bottom rail. If you are using tongue-and-groove siding, position the first

board so the groove faces down. Slip the tongue of the second board up into it, and so on.

4 **Attaching the Kickboard.** You can choose to nail a 1x8 or 1x10 kickboard along the bottom rail to cover the gap and discourage animals from digging under the fence. If so, leave the bottom ¾ inch of the rail exposed when attaching the siding. Notch the kickboard to fit around any concrete collars. Nail it to the exposed section of bottom rail. Pressure-treated kickboards can be placed on the ground, but are more effective when they extend 6 to 8 inches into the ground. Dig a trench while digging the posts if the kickboard will be set in the ground.

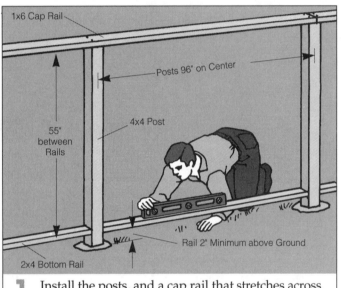

1 Install the posts, and a cap rail that stretches across at least three posts. Cut the bottom rail to fit.

2 The center support gives the fence rigidity. Slip a block underneath it to support it when nailing.

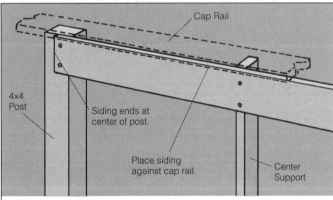

3 Attach siding boards that reach from the center of one post to the center of another. The fence will be stronger if the boards span at least two posts.

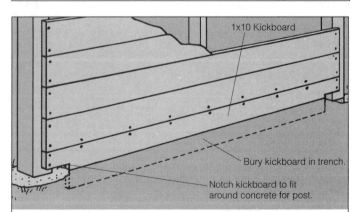

4 The optional kickboard will keep animals from slipping under the fence. Use pressure-treated wood, and cut it to fit around any obstructions.

Making a Vertical Board-on-Board Fence

This 72-inch fence provides some privacy while not completely blocking sunshine and wind. It works well along a property line because both sides have siding. The fence is covered with 1x6 siding boards, spaced one board width, or 5½ inches, apart. Note in the drawing how boards are staggered: A gap on one side of the fence is partially blocked by a board on the other side.

1 **Building the Framework.** Set the posts 60½ inches apart. This spacing allows for six 1x6 siding boards, spaced one board apart. Alter to fit your needs, but the maximum distance between posts should be no more than 96 inches. Cut 2x4 rails to fit between the posts. Position them so that you'll be nailing the siding into the wide face of the rail. Center the rails on the face of the post. Fence brackets will make positioning easier. The top rail can be attached flush with the top of the

posts, as shown, or several inches below it, depending on the effect you want to achieve.

2 **Attaching the Boards to the Front Side.** Drill two pilot holes

to avoid splitting the siding boards at each rail location. Butt the rail against the end post and attach the first 1x6 board to the rails with galvanized 8d nails or 2-inch deck screws. Then, using a 1x6 block as a spacer, attach

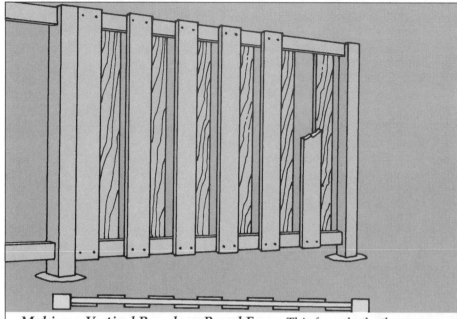

Making a Vertical Board-on-Board Fence. This fence looks the same on both sides, so it's a good choice for marking property lines. The boards are spaced one board-width apart; for more privacy, reduce the spacing.

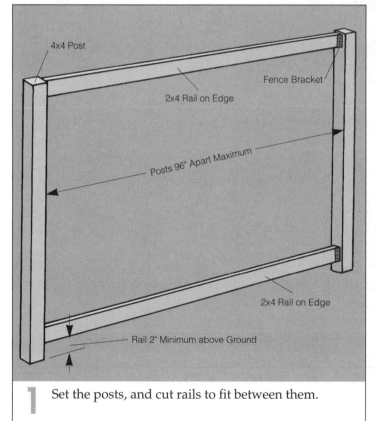

1 Set the posts, and cut rails to fit between them.

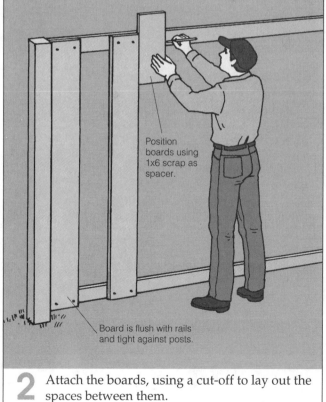

2 Attach the boards, using a cut-off to lay out the spaces between them.

the next boards to the front side of the fence. Lay out the spacing with a piece of 1x6 scrap as shown. If necessary, adjust the spacing so that there's no more than a full board width between the last board and the post. Use a carpenter's level to make sure the boards are plumb as you attach them.

3 **Attaching the Boards to the Back Side.** On the other side of the fence, temporarily tack one of the boards to the rail so that it is snug against the post; this will be the spacer board. Butt a second board against the first and attach it to the rails. Remove the first board and use it as a spacer to attach remaining boards. Adjust the spacing if needed, and check for plumb.

Installing an Alternating Panel Fence

This variation of a solid-board fence has 1x6 boards to the neighbor's side of the fence from the middle of the span to one post and on your side of the fence between the middle and the next post. It enables you to share an attractive fence with your neighbors while providing privacy and good wind control. The fence shown has posts set on 96-inch centers with top rails fastened to the post tops. Bottom rails are toe-nailed between posts. The fence is 72 inches tall, which is typical of boundary fences. You can build it lower if desired.

1 **Building the Framework.** Set the posts and install the rails. Attach a 2x4 center support midway between each pair of posts, as shown. Drive two 16d nails or 3-inch galvanized deck screws through the top rail into the center support, and screw or toenail two 10d nails through the support into the bottom rail. Put a block under the bottom rail while you're nailing, and make sure the center support is square to the rails.

2 **Filling in the First Panel.** Position the first board so that it covers the post. Drill two pilot holes

Spacer Temporarily Tacked in Place

Nail this board permanently in place.

3 Attach boards to the other side of the fence. Start by temporarily nailing a board next to the post, then permanently nailing another board next to it.

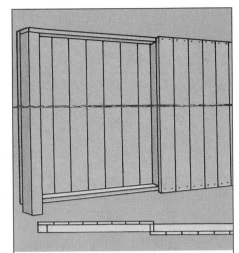

Installing an Alternating-Panel Fence. This solid fence looks the same from both sides. The alternating panels create a textured surface.

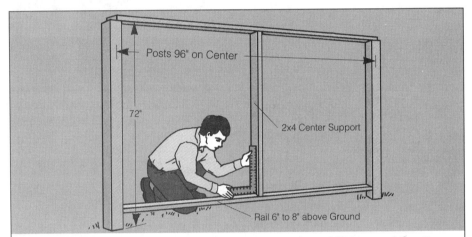

Posts 96" on Center

72"

2x4 Center Support

Rail 6" to 8" above Ground

1 Set the posts and rails, and attach a center support between the rails. Make sure the center support is square to the rails.

1x6 Siding Spaced ⅛" Apart

2 Attach boards to one side of the fence. With a carpenter's level, make sure the boards are plumb.

at rail heights, and fasten the board with 8d galvanized nails or 2-inch deck screws. With a carpenter's level, make sure the board is plumb. When you add the remaining boards, space them so that the last one will be set flush with the edge of the center support. Leave ⅛ inch between boards. If necessary, rip the last board to width using a table saw, or circular saw.

3 Attaching the Alternate Panel. Move to the rails between the center support and the next post. Cross to the other side of the fence, and attach 1x6 siding boards to it. When finished, work your way down the length of the fence, alternating sides between sets of posts.

Building a Louver Fence

Although a louver fence requires more lumber than a conventional board fence, it makes an attractive enclosure for patios and pools. A louver fence filters sunshine and wind without completely blocking them; this fence also offers privacy. Louvers are commonly set at 45 degrees, although you can set them at another angle to provide more (or less) privacy and wind control. The fence shown here is just over 72 inches tall and has posts set on 96-inch centers. The louvers are 1x4 boards nailed at an angle to 2x4 rails. Before nailing, check the effects of different louver angles by tacking or clamping a few boards in position. You can tailor the angle to your needs—for example, to see in and out at one end of your yard and have complete privacy at the other end.

1 Cutting the Louvers. Build the framework, set posts, and cut the rails to fit. Note the rails are different lengths: The bottom rail is dadoed into the posts, while the top rail sits on top of them. After building the framework, cut the fence boards to fit between the top and bottom rails.

2 Attaching the First Louver. Put the first louver between the rails near a post. Set it at the proper angle with the 45-degree face of a combin-

3 Repeat the same process on the opposite side of the frame, alternating down the line of posts.

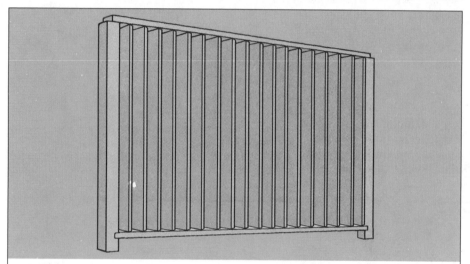

Building a Louver Fence. With boards installed at an angle, this fence filters wind and sunlight. Louvers can be installed horizontally as well.

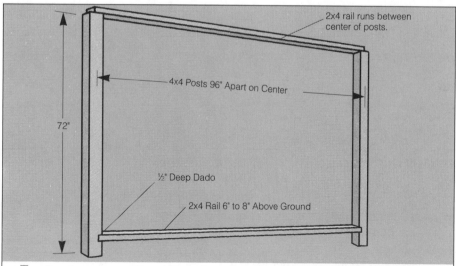

2x4 rail runs between center of posts.

4x4 Posts 96" Apart on Center

72"

½" Deep Dado

2x4 Rail 6" to 8" Above Ground

1 Set the posts and cut the rails to fit. Then cut the fence boards to fit between the top and bottom rails.

ation square or speed square. Center the louver on rail so that any gap between the louver and rail edges is uniform. Slide the square until the louver butts against the post. Double check the angle and mark the location by tracing a line along the louver. Drill pilot holes and toenail the first louver to the bottom rail with 10d galvanized finish nails. Drive two 2½-inch screws or nails through the top rail into the angled louver.

3 **Making a Spacer.** For accurate spacing and angling of the boards, make a spacer block by cutting one end of a 1x3 scrap to the desired angle. (This spacer block will space the boards 2½ inches apart. If you want wider spaces, use a 1x4 block; use a 1x2 block for thinner spaces.) Lay the spacer block on the bottom rail with the mitered end flush with the edge of the rail, and guide each board into position.

4 **Attaching the Remaining Louvers.** Attach the remaining louvers between the posts to fill out the section. Put a block under the bottom rail to keep it steady as you toenail. Adjust the spacing of the last few louvers to allow enough room for the final louver.

Making a Lattice-Top Fence

Board-and-lattice fences offer privacy and good wind protection while retaining an open feeling. The lattice-top fence shown looks the same on both sides. It uses prefab 12 by 96-inch lattice panels sandwiched between 1x1 strips on the top and middle rails. The 4x4 posts are set on 96-inch centers, and the lattice is cut to fit between posts. Use an old saw blade and wear eye protection because your saw is bound to hit the staples that hold together prefab lattice panels. The bottom portion of the fence consists of 1x8 boards centered between the posts and rails, also held in place with 1x1 strips. For a nicer appearance, you can substitute tongue-and-groove boards for square-edged ones.

2 Slide the first louver against the post, and adjust its angle with the 45 degree face of a combination or speed square.

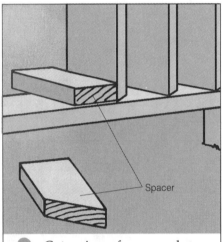

3 Cut a piece of scrap and use it as a spacer to position the remaining louvers.

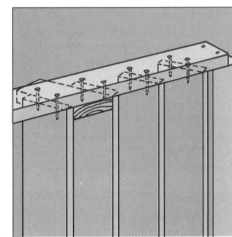

4 Attach the remaining louvers with nails or screws in the top. Toenail louvers to the bottom rail.

Making a Lattice-Top Fence. This is another fence that looks the same from both sides. The prefab lattice top panel makes it less imposing than a solid-board privacy fence.

1 Building the Frame. Attach the bottom and middle rails to the posts so that the top edge of the middle rail is 12 inches below the post top. For the 72-inch-high fence shown here, the distance between the middle rail and the bottom rail should be 53½ inches—enough to leave a 2-inch gap between the ground and the bottom rail.

2 Attaching the 1x1 Strips and Boards. Attach four 1x1 strips (available at most lumberyards) to the rails and posts with 6d nails so that the strips are set back about ⅝ inch from the faces of the posts and rails. The strip corners can be butted, or, for a better appearance, mitered. Predrill nail holes near the ends to avoid splitting.

Starting flush against one post, attach the boards as shown by toenailing through them into the rails with 8d galvanized finish nails. Leave ½-inch spaces between the boards or space evenly so that the last board is a full one. If you need to, rip the last board to width on a table saw. After filling in each section, attach a second set of 1x1 strips set back ⅝ inches from the opposite side of the fence.

3 Attaching the Top Rails and Lattice. Nail the 2x4 top rails with 16d galvanized nails across the post tops; 96-inch 2x4s should reach from the center of one post to the center of the next. With 6d galvanized finishing nails, attach one set of 1x1 strips to the inside of the posts and to the top and middle rail, positioned so there is 1 inch between the strip and the front of the rail. Trim the ends of the lattice strips to fit between the posts. Place the lattice against the strips, then install a second set of strips to hold the lattice in place. It is not necessary to nail the lattice to the strips.

Picket Fences

Picket fences are often found gracing the front yards of Colonial, Victorian, and other traditionally styled houses.

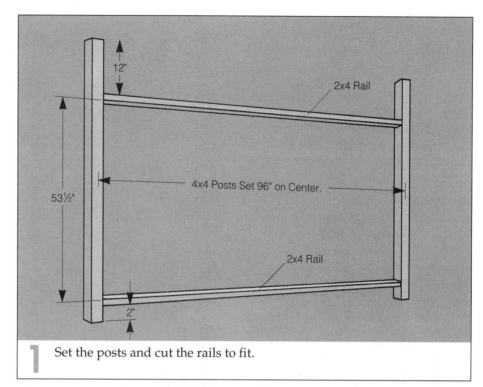

1 Set the posts and cut the rails to fit.

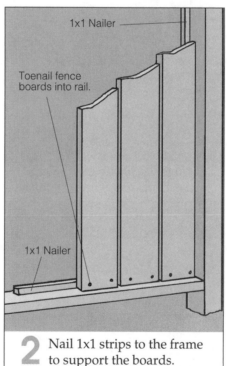

2 Nail 1x1 strips to the frame to support the boards.

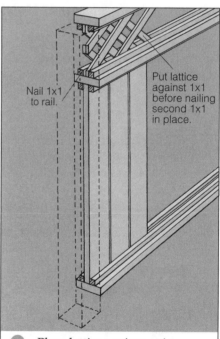

3 Place lattice against strip. Attach a second set of 1x1 strips to hold the lattice in place.

They are appropriate for almost any house. As opposed to solid-board fences, the open design shows off plantings within the yard, yet provides a definite boundary to discourage casual trespassers.

Planting low shrubs, vines, or perennial plants, such as red roses, next to the fence helps soften the repetitive design, although you'll need to prune plants back when it comes time to repaint the fence. There is a wide range of picket and post-top treatments that can give each fence an individual character while retaining a traditional design.

Picket-Top Designs

Some lumberyards and home centers carry precut pickets, but the designs are often limited. To make your own simple pointed pickets, clamp two or three boards together and cut the tops with a hand saw or circular saw. To make fancier top cuts, clamp together a pair of boards and cut the pattern with a saber saw.

Many lumberyards also sell precut posts with decorative tops. Some of these tops, called finials, embellish the classical beauty of a picket fence; lumberyards sell separate finials, too, that can be attached to 4x4 or 6x6 posts. If you have access to a band saw, you can cut your own post top designs. A few examples of post and picket tops are shown in this section.

Building a Basic Picket Fence

Most picket fences are 36 to 48 inches tall, and use a framework of 4x4 posts on 96-inch centers with 2x4 rails, just like the board fences on the previous pages. On some designs, the posts extend above the picket tops, in which case you can use a decorative post top. On other designs, the top rails are attached across the post tops, and the pickets extend 4 to 6 inches above the framework.

The pickets themselves usually consist of evenly spaced 1x3s or 1x4s attached to the outside of the rails. A couple of tips: The pickets should always be the same width as the posts. The bottoms of the pickets should be at least 2 inches above the ground level to prevent decay and make it easier both to paint the fence and to remove weeds.

1 **Building the Frame.** Build the frame so the bottom rail fits between the posts, and the top rail overlaps the posts. For strength, use a top rail that spans at least three posts. Cut the rail so that it meets the next rail in the center of a post. Cut the 1x4 pickets so that they will extend about 6 inches above the top rail.

Picket-Top Designs. The look of a fence depends on the style of the pickets. Pickets can be customized or bought precut at lumberyards.

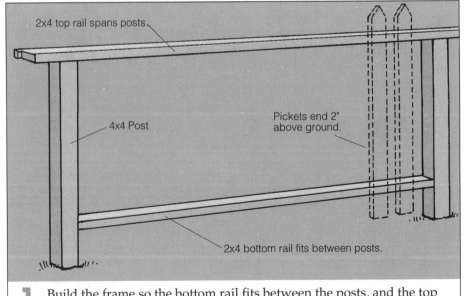

2x4 top rail spans posts.

4x4 Post

Pickets end 2" above ground.

2x4 bottom rail fits between posts.

1 Build the frame so the bottom rail fits between the posts, and the top rail overlaps the posts.

2 Attaching the Post Pickets.

Starting at one end of the fence, attach the first picket to the end post with two 6d galvanized nails or two 2-inch galvanized deck screws at the same height as the rails. Make sure the edge of the picket is flush with the edge of the post, as shown. Install a picket over every post in the fence.

3 Spacing the Pickets Evenly.

The best picket fences have uniformly spaced pickets. You can get uniform spacing with some simple math. First, choose the number of pickets you want between the posts. Multiply the number by the width of a picket to find out the total distance occupied by pickets. (Round up to a whole number, if necessary.) Subtract the answer from the distance between posts to find out how much unoccupied space there is.

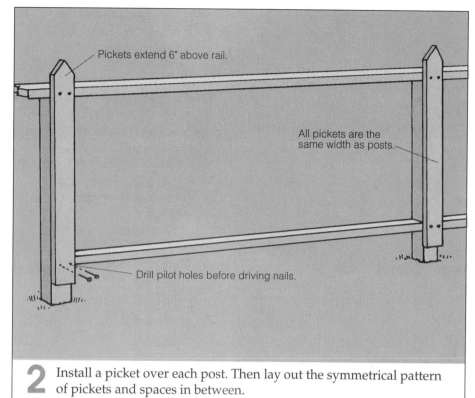

Pickets extend 6" above rail.

All pickets are the same width as posts.

Drill pilot holes before driving nails.

2 Install a picket over each post. Then lay out the symmetrical pattern of pickets and spaces in between.

Making a Curved-Top Picket Fence

The undulating shape of a curved-top picket fence nicely complements a natural setting or a gingerbread house style. You should make the curved top by cutting the pickets after they've been fastened to the fence frame. The only pickets that should be cut to their exact length are the post pickets; you can let the intervening pickets run wild as long as they extend at least 6 inches above the top rail and are even along the bottom.

You will need soft, heavy rope cut about 12 inches longer than the span between posts. Attach the rope to the top of the post pickets, allowing it to sag freely across the picket faces. After making sure that the rope does not sag below the top rail, carefully trace the rope on all of the picket faces except the post pickets. Remove the rope, cut along the line with a saber saw, and sand the picket tops smooth. For a finished appearance, top off the posts with decorative caps or finials, available at lumberyards and home centers.

Tape rope to pickets and trace along it to lay out curve.

Finials accent finished curve.

To find out the space between pickets, divide the amount of unoccupied space by the number of spaces per section. The total number of spaces will be one more than the total number of pickets.

4 Attaching the Remaining Pickets. Rip a board to the width you just computed and use it to space the pickets. A wood cleat nailed to the top of the spacer board makes it easier to use.

Set up stakes and a level string 2 inches above ground, and set the pickets to this height. Place the spacer board against a post picket, then butt the second picket against the board and nail or screw it in place. Repeat for remaining pickets, checking them for plumb with a carpenter's level. Make sure the spacing will work by marking the last few boards and spaces on the rails and spreading any discrepancy over several pickets.

Other Wood Fences

In addition to the board-fence designs shown so far, wood can be used in other ways to create attractive fences. The following pages show some of the more popular types.

Making a Rustic Post-and-Rail Fence

If you're looking for a fence that works well on uneven terrain, and has rustic charm, a rail fence is a good choice.

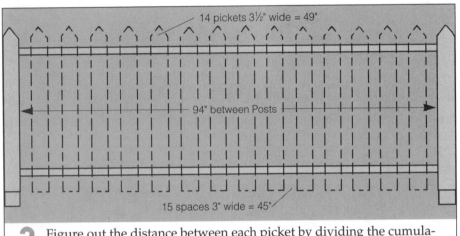

14 pickets 3½" wide = 49"

94" between Posts

15 spaces 3" wide = 45"

3 Figure out the distance between each picket by dividing the cumulative space between pickets by the number of spaces.

Post   Rails

Rails butt in mortise.

Rails overlap.

Making a Rustic Post-and-Rail Fence. Rails fit into a mortise in the post. They can be butted together, overlapped, or tenoned.

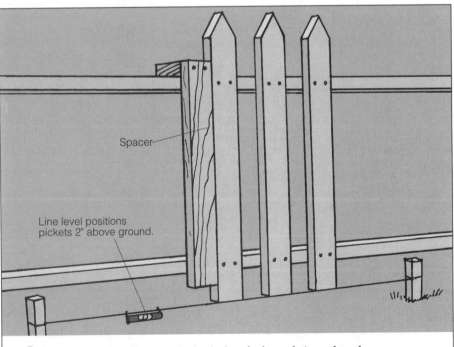

Spacer

Line level positions pickets 2" above ground.

4 Position the pickets with the help of a board ripped to the proper width, and nail the pickets in place. Using a spacer saves repetitive measuring and assures uniformity.

Rails are readily available at lumberyards and garden centers. The rails may be square or roughly wedge-shaped, just like a piece of firewood, and are typically from 72 to 96 inches long. In some areas, round, unsplit "palings" are available, with or without the bark attached.

Rails generally fit into a mortise in the post. They can overlap, they can be tenoned, or they can simply butt together. Fences with two or three rails per section are the most common. Some lumberyards carry premortised posts and tenoned rails, sold as kits, or you can buy the rough stock and cut your own mortises and tenons.

1 **Mortising the Posts.** Use a pencil and a try square to mark the size and locations of the mortises. Rail fences are somewhat crude (which is part of their rustic charm), so you don't need to be too exact. Make the width and length of the mortise ⅛ to ¼ inch larger than the width and thickness of the rails. Cut the mortises in the same locations on each post: Make the top edge of each upper mortise about 2 inches below the post top, for example. Lay out the bottom mortise so that bottom rail will be at least 6 inches above ground level after the post is set. To rough out the mortise, drill a series of 1-inch holes all the way through the post, then clean up the edges with a hammer and wide wood chisel.

2 **Cutting Tenons in the Rails.** With a hand saw, cut half-tenons in the rail ends so that they overlap in the mortise. Cut tenons about 1 inch shorter than the width of the post. Tenons are not required where the rails join the end posts. For corner posts, cut mortises as shown.

3 **Erecting the Fence.** Set the first post, then set the next post loosely in place. Insert the rails, plumb and set the post permanently, and repeat the process.

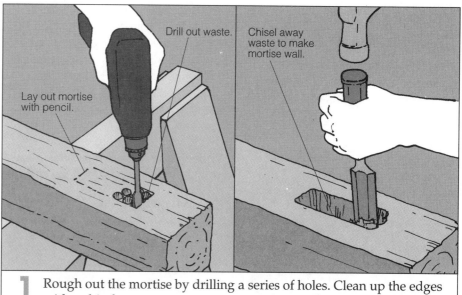

1 Rough out the mortise by drilling a series of holes. Clean up the edges with a chisel.

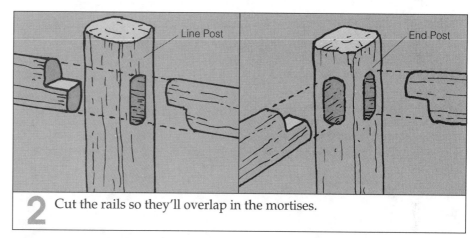

2 Cut the rails so they'll overlap in the mortises.

3 Set one post firmly, put in the rails, and then slip the second post over them.

Making a Formal Post-and-Rail Fence

Formal post-and-rail fences use dimensional lumber, typically 4x4s for the posts, and 2x6s or 4x4s for the rails. Depending on the fence height and look you want to achieve, you

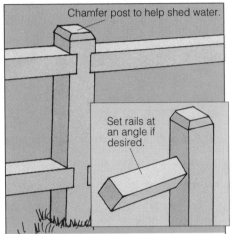

Making a Formal Post-and-Rail Fence. A post-and-rail fence made of dimensioned lumber has a more formal look.

can attach one, two, or even three rails between the posts. Rails are either toenailed between posts or dadoed into them. The dado joint in this fence design provides a strong connection and is easier to make than the mortise-and-tenon joint used in the rustic post and rail fence. The fence will have a more finished appearance and will shed water if you chamfer the post tops, as shown.

1 **Setting the Posts.** Cut 1½-inch-deep dadoes in the posts (see "Dadoing Posts" on page 29). Dado adjacent sides of the corner posts. Set the posts to the same height on 96-inch centers. With a line level, make sure the dadoes in the posts are aligned properly.

2 **Adding the Rails.** Cut the rails to length, and slip them into the dadoes, tapping lightly with a hammer, if necessary, to fit them in place. Secure by toenailing two 10d-galvanized nails through the predrilled rails. Where two rails meet

at a corner, you will have to notch one of the rails to fit into the dado. Install the first rail, then notch one side of the second one to fit into the adjacent dado. (If your design calls for butting the rails between posts, you won't have to notch the corners.)

Installing a Post-and-Board Fence

Because of their low, open design, post-and-board fences define boundaries while still providing good views from both sides of the fence. They are also easy to build and use less lumber than most other fences. This type of fence commonly consists of two, three, or four 1x4 or 1x6 rails nailed to one side of the posts. Most residential versions are 36 to 48 inches high. Posts are typically spaced on 72-inch centers for one-by rails or 96-inch centers for two-by rails, with the rails spanning three or four posts. Joints between top and bottom rails are staggered.

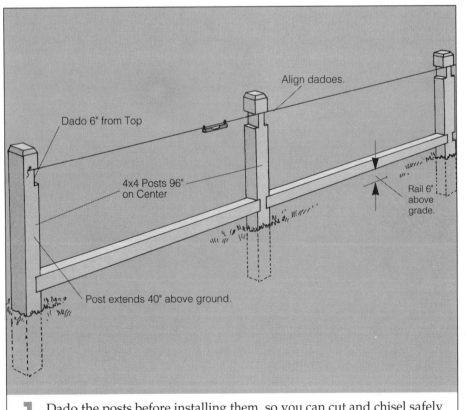

1 Dado the posts before installing them, so you can cut and chisel safely and accurately. Check the alignment with twine and a line level.

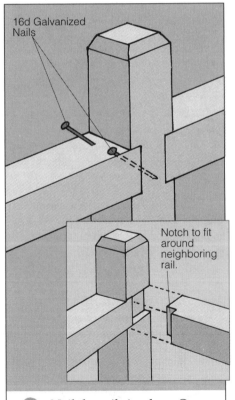

2 Nail the rails in place. On corner posts, cut a notch in one rail to house the other rail.

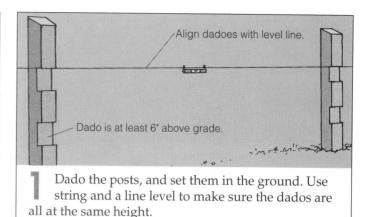

Align dadoes with level line.

Dado is at least 6" above grade.

1 Dado the posts, and set them in the ground. Use string and a line level to make sure the dados are all at the same height.

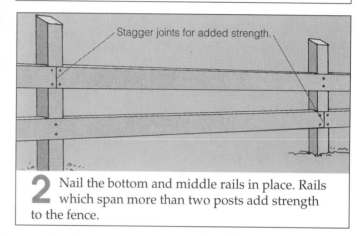

Stagger joints for added strength.

2 Nail the bottom and middle rails in place. Rails which span more than two posts add strength to the fence.

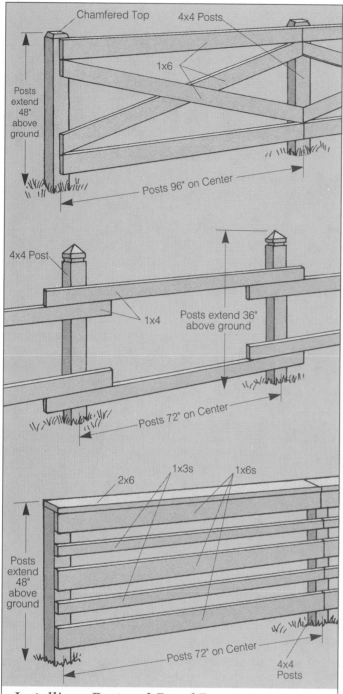

Chamfered Top

4x4 Posts

1x6

Posts extend 48" above ground

Posts 96" on Center

4x4 Post

1x4

Posts extend 36" above ground

Posts 72" on Center

2x6

1x3s

1x6s

Posts extend 48" above ground

Posts 72" on Center

4x4 Posts

Installing a Post-and-Board Fence. Shown here are a few of the many post-and-board fences. For a sturdier fence, you can substitute 2-inch-thick boards for the 1-inch-thick boards shown.

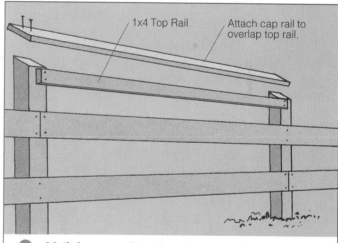

1x4 Top Rail

Attach cap rail to overlap top rail.

3 Nail the top rail in place, and install the cap rail so that the two are flush. If desired, post tops can be angled to provide a slanted cap that sheds water.

1 **Preparing and Setting the Posts.** In the fence shown, the center and bottom rails are dadoed into 4x4 posts. Position the dadoes so that the boards will be spaced equally. The bottom board should be at least 6 inches above grade. Set the posts at equal heights on 72-inch centers.

2 **Installing the Middle and Bottom Rails.** Cut the 1x6 rails to length, and attach them to the posts with 8d galvanized nails or 2-inch galvanized all-purpose screws. For extra strength, you can cut the rails 12 feet long (to span three posts), then stagger the rail ends so that joints do not occur on the same post, as shown.

3 **Adding the Top Rail and Cap.** Fasten the 1x4 top rail even with the tops of the posts. Fasten the 1x6 cap board to the post tops so that it is flush with the front of the top rail.

Use four 10d nails or 2½-inch deck screws at each post. If desired, you can angle the post tops to provide a slanted cap that sheds water and keeps youngsters from walking on top of the fence.

Building a Plywood Fence

Plywood fences create a solid, opaque barrier that provides much the same privacy as a masonry wall. You should use only exterior-grade plywood (designated "ext") for these fences. Plywood with an "X" in its name, such as CDX, is not meant for outdoor use; the "X" simply means that the plywood may be left exposed for a short while until it is covered with house-siding materials such as shingles or stucco. A popular type of exterior plywood, T1-11, has channels routed in the face to mimic tongue-and-groove boards.

Even exterior-grade plywood can peel apart, so protect the edges with caulk and 1x4 battens. You should also install a 1x6 cap board to protect the top edges.

Plywood fences usually look best painted to match your house. They also can be covered with other materials, such as stucco or shingles. The plywood is typically ⅝- or ¾-inch thick 4x8 panels. If the fence is subject to strong winds, a fence 48 inches high should have 4x6 posts set at least 24 inches into concrete collars in the ground.

1 **Building the Frame.** The fence shown here consists of 4x4 posts set at equal heights on 96-inch centers. The 2x4 top and bottom rails are installed with the wide dimension up. A third rail is centered between them, also with the wide dimension up. Attach the framework with galvanized 10d nails or 2-inch deck screws.

2 **Adding the Panels.** With a helper, attach ¾-inch, 4x8 plywood panels to the fence frame, using 8d galvanized nails or 1½-inch galvanized deck screws, spaced

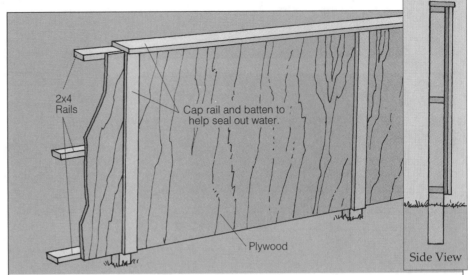

2x4 Rails — *Cap rail and batten to help seal out water.* — *Plywood* — *Side View*

Building a Plywood Fence. An economical solid fence, this plywood fence can be painted or covered with house-siding materials, such as shingles or stucco.

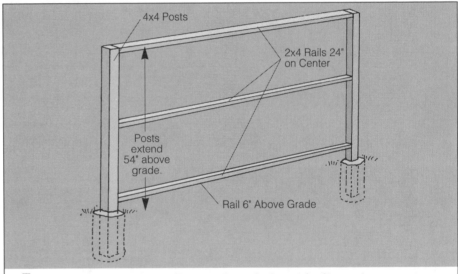

4x4 Posts — *2x4 Rails 24" on Center* — *Posts extend 54" above grade.* — *Rail 6" Above Grade*

1 Set the posts, and install 2x4 rails with the wide dimension up.

Using Other Panels

You can substitute fiberglass or various types of plastic panels for plywood. These panels come in a variety of thicknesses, colors, surface textures, and degrees of translucency or opacity (ability to transmit light). These panels, however require careful placement to protect them from the weather.

The thickness of the panels you choose depends on their overall size; the larger the panel, the thicker it must be to withstand winds. Large (4x6 or 4x8 foot) sheets may require additional bracing within the fence to prevent excessive flexing in high wind conditions.

Although you can cut plastic and fiberglass panels with a fine-tooth hand saw, a band saw, or a table saw equipped with a fine-tooth blade, it is easier to have the dealer precut the panels.

about 6 inches apart. Start at one top corner and work your way across. Do the same for the next panel. Leave a ⅛-inch gap between the panels.

3 Adding the Battens and Cap.
Attach the 1x6 cap board so that it's flush with the back edge of the post. Caulk the ⅛-inch gap between plywood panels with a good exterior latex or silicone caulk. Nail 1x4 battens over the gaps with 6d galvanized finishing nails. Set the nail heads and fill the holes with exterior-grade wood putty. Nail a second batten to the end posts as shown in the inset.

Making a Wood-and-Wire Fence

Welded- or woven-wire mesh can be attached to a wood frame to make an attractive, lightweight, and economical fence. Low wire fences are an excellent choice for enclosing children's play areas or defining garden areas; a taller fence provides security and can act as a trellis for climbing vines.

Welded wire comes in a variety of gauges and mesh sizes, typically in 36-, 48-, and 72-inch widths, in 50- or 100-foot rolls. It is best to choose the heaviest-gauge wire available; lightweight wire is easily deformed and prone to rust. Most wood-and-wire fences use a 2x2- or 2x4-inch welded-wire mesh, either galvanized or vinyl-coated. Vinyl-coated wire comes in a limited range of colors: White and forest green are the most common. Green blends well into the landscape, making the fence nearly invisible; use white when you want to define an area or provide contrast to surrounding landscape features.

Because the wood-and-wire fence shown here is more than 48 inches high, it has a center rail for extra stability. Fences less than 48 inches high don't require a center rail. You can add a pressure-treated kickboard to keep children and animals from crawling underneath the fence; the 1x6 cap board is optional but recommended to cover exposed wire tips.

2 Attach plywood to the rails with nails or screws.

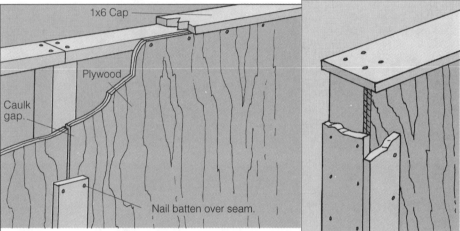

1x6 Cap

Plywood

Caulk gap.

Nail batten over seam.

3 Cover the edges of the plywood with a top batten, and with another batten at the seams between the plywood.

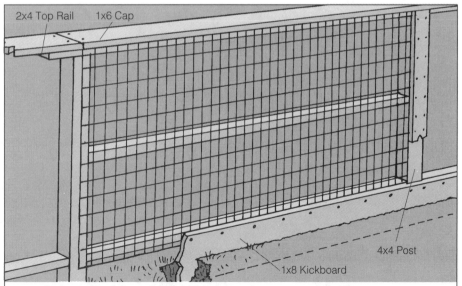

2x4 Top Rail · 1x6 Cap

4x4 Post

1x8 Kickboard

Making a Wood-and-Wire Fence. This fence is a good choice for enclosing children's play areas because you can see through it. Be sure to cover all wire ends with battens, a cap board, and a kickboard.

1 **Building the Frame.** Construct the framework with 4x4 posts spaced on 96-inch centers, and 2x4 top and bottom rails. Position the rails so the distance between the top of the top rail and the bottom of the bottom rail is 48 inches. Fasten the top rail to the post tops. Fasten the bottom rail between posts.

2 **Attach the wire.** With a helper, unroll enough wire to cover the first fence section. Hold the end about 1 inch back from the edge of the post, and align the top edge of the wire with the top rail. Fasten the top corner with a ¾-inch U-staple. While your helper holds the wire even with the top rail, staple the wire every 6 inches, first working your way down the post, then across the top rail, followed by the bottom rail and the next post. Have your helper stretch more wire across the next section, and repeat the stapling process.

3 **Splicing the Wire.** If you run out of wire before you reach the end of the fence, cut back the wire to the nearest post. Start the new roll by overlapping the ends. When you reach the end of the fence, cut the wire 1 inch short of the edge of the post and staple down the ends.

4 **Adding the Battens.** Adding 1x4 battens to the posts gives the fence a finished appearance, helps secure the wire to the posts, and covers any protruding wire ends. Cut battens to span from the bottom to the top rail, and attach with 8d galvanized nails or 2-inch galvanized deck screws. Add a 1x6 cap board to protect the batten ends.

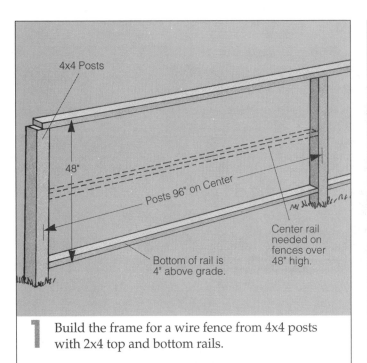

4x4 Posts

48"

Posts 96" on Center

Center rail needed on fences over 48" high.

Bottom of rail is 4" above grade.

1 Build the frame for a wire fence from 4x4 posts with 2x4 top and bottom rails.

¾" staples hold mesh in place.

2 Unroll the fence and staple it to a post. Staple along the top rail to the next post; then staple the bottom rail before nailing fence wire to the next post.

3 If you run out of wire, splice it at the nearest post, and staple down loose ends.

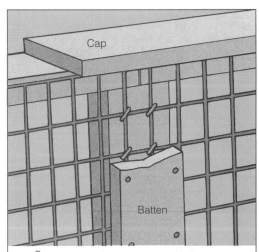

Cap

Batten

4 Optional battens cover the posts and the top of the fence.

INSTALLING METAL & VINYL FENCES

Obviously, not all fences are made of wood. The three most popular fence alternatives are ornamental metal fences, vinyl fences, and chain link fences. There is also a variety of simple, temporary fences that use a combination of wood and other materials.

A note of caution concerning chain link fences: Installation requires some special equipment. Low chain link fences are easy to install. For taller fences, consider hiring a qualified fence contractor to install the fence. Most retail outlets that carry chain link fence supplies also offer installation services.

Ornamental Metal Fences

The earliest ornamental metal fences were made of wrought iron that was hammered on anvils and twisted into classic forms. Although a few craftsmen still work in wrought iron, most ornamental metal fencing today is made of cast iron, tubular steel, or aluminum. You can choose from a variety of prefabricated designs and install the fence yourself, or you can have a fence custom-made and installed by contractors.

Installing a Prefabricated Metal Fence

Prefabricated metal fences are sold through fence suppliers who also deliver the fence to your home and install it. Styles range from ornate Victorian reproductions to sleek, modern designs. Most companies that make prefabricated fences also offer matching gates and the hardware necessary to mount them.

Most prefabricated steel and aluminum fences come with a durable factory-applied finish, typically a polyester powder coating. Colors commonly available include black, white, or brown. Check the manufacturer's warranty to see how long the fence is guaranteed against rust and corrosion. If the fence you choose requires on-site painting, use a high-quality, rust-resistant paint. It is easier to paint the components before installing them.

Post Options. With a helper or two, prefab metal fences are easy to install. The prefabricated panels typically come in 72- to 96-inch lengths (and various heights) and fit neatly into prepunched holes in the metal posts. You can also buy prefabricated sections and attach them to wood posts or masonry columns with mounting brackets (supplied by the manufacturer), lag screws, and masonry anchors.

No matter which route you go, spacing between posts depends on the size of

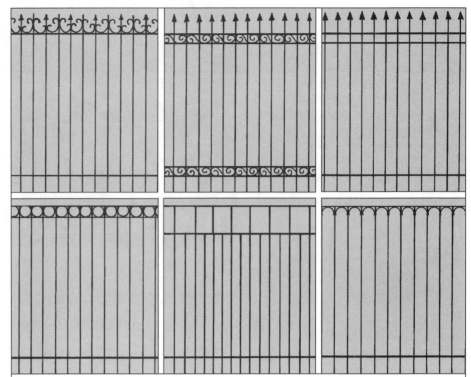

Ornamental Metal Fences. Shown are several popular styles of prefabricated ornamental metal fence sections.

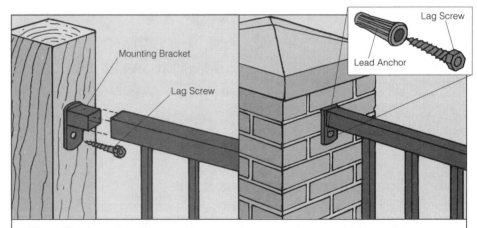

Post Options. Manufacturers provide special brackets for attaching metal fence sections to wood posts or masonry columns.

the prefab panels, which must fit snugly between them. For this reason, it is best to erect the fence section by section, attaching prefab panels after two posts are in place. Use these instructions along with those provided by the manufacturer for the specific fence you are installing.

1 Locating and Digging the Postholes. Carefully lay out the postholes according to the length of the prefab panels and prefab

gate, if you're using one. Then dig the postholes. If you're planning to install a custom-built gate, you can set the posts and build the gate to fit the opening. For more information on layout, see "Plotting Fences" on page 12.

In warm climates, postholes for metal fences 48 inches or less should be at least 18 inches deep. For 60-inch fences, dig holes 24 inches deep. For 72-inch or taller fences, dig holes

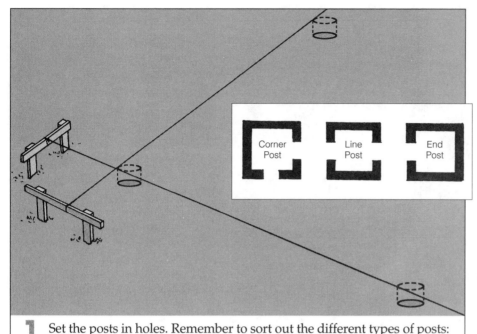

Setting the First Post. In most cases, you set the posts one at a time, filling in panels as you go. If post caps are provided, install them before setting the posts in the ground. Starting at one end or corner, set the first post in concrete. (To speed things up, you can use a fast-setting concrete mix.) Set the post all the way into the hole, positioning it along the line you set up to lay out postholes. After a few minutes, raise the post to the correct level. Make sure the holes that hold the fence sections clear the ground enough to allow installation. The exact height varies among manufacturers, so check the instructions that come with the fence. Temporarily brace the fence posts until the concrete sets, and check frequently with a level to make sure the posts remain plumb.

1 Set the posts in holes. Remember to sort out the different types of posts: for corners, ends, and the line posts in between.

Drive end caps into post before setting post.

30 inches deep. In cold climates, set the concrete below the frost line.

Before installing the posts, separate them according to function: Line posts have holes punched on opposite sides to accommodate the fence sections; end posts have only one side punched; corner posts are punched on adjacent sides.

3 **Installing the Fence Sections.** After the concrete sets slightly for the first post, install a second post, then insert the rails of the first prefab section into the holes punched in the first post. Slide the rails into the holes in the second post. Attach with the screws, rings, or clips provided by the manufacturer. Check the posts and first section for plumb and level, then install the third post and second fence

Concrete extends below frost line. Minimum depth is 18".

2 Check with your building department about frost depth and footing requirements.

Set first post plumb.

Slide rails into post and set second post plumb.

3 Work your way down the fence, first installing a post, then a fence section, followed by a post and then another section. The fence sections attach with clips or screws supplied by the manufacturer.

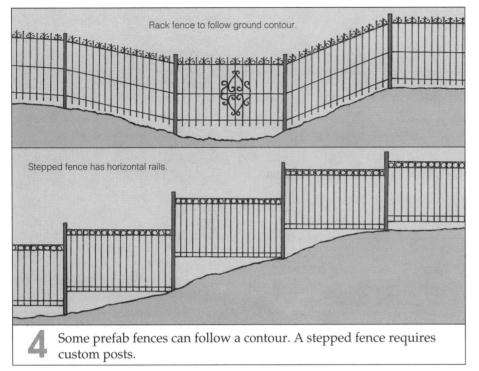

Rack fence to follow ground contour.

Stepped fence has horizontal rails.

4 Some prefab fences can follow a contour. A stepped fence requires custom posts.

Vinyl Fences

These prefabricated fences are made of PVC plastic, the same material as vinyl siding, although fence material is usually a heavier gauge. Vinyl fences imitate a wide variety of fence styles, including board, rail, picket, lattice, and ornamental metal. A few of the more popular designs are shown.

Vinyl fencing must be ordered directly from manufacturers or their distributors. The fences come in limited colors—usually white, brown, and tan. Since the color runs throughout the material, however, vinyl fences never need painting. They won't rust, decay, or peel and they're impervious to wood-boring insects. Although vinyl fences are more expensive than the same styles in wood, the manufacturers say their higher initial cost should be offset by longer life and lower maintenance costs.

Usually you buy the fence material in kit form, with precut posts, rails, and siding. The rails fit into mortises or holes cut into the hollow posts and are secured with screws, clips, or lock rings. The rails are also hollow and may be channeled to accept simulated boards or mortised to accept pickets.

section. Continue in this fashion for successive sections.

4 **Dealing with Special Situations.** If the last section of fencing in your layout is shorter than the panel you want to use, cut the rails shorter with a hacksaw. If the prefab rail ends are notched, cut similar notches to fit into the holes that are punched in the posts.

Many prefab panels can be racked to follow gentle contours and slopes. For steep slopes, you can order 45-degree sections with posts designed to accept them. If the fence follows a contour, set all the posts at the same height above ground. If you are building a stepped fence, you will probably need posts of varying lengths. These posts usually must be custom-made, not prefabricated.

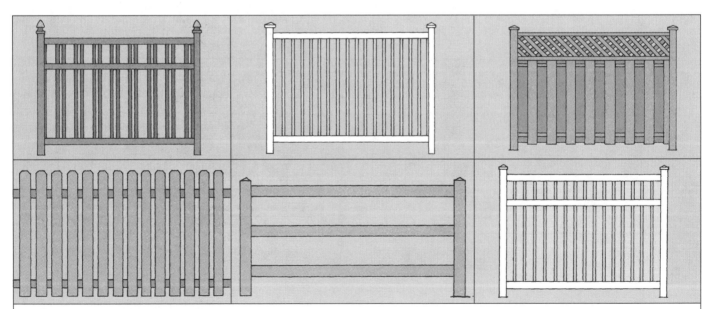

Vinyl Fences. Vinyl fences are manufactured to look like wood or metal, but they require less maintenance. Several other styles are available.

Building a Vinyl Fence

Use these directions along with the manufacturer's assembly instructions to install your fence. Many manufacturers also provide matching gates and mounting hardware. The components usually come in precut lengths, but you can cut them with a fine-tooth hand saw.

1 Assembling the Rails and Pickets. In the design shown, pickets or boards are fitted into slots cut in bottom and top rails. For easier handling, use a wood support stand to help you assemble the sections. Foam inserts plug the open ends of the rail sections. If inserts are not provided, cover each rail end with a piece of duct tape. In a few designs, PVC cement may be required to secure various components.

2 Installing the Posts. Lay out and dig postholes. Most manufacturers recommend a 12-inch diameter hole. The depth of the hole is determined by the fence height and is also recommended by the fence manufacturer. Place a 4-inch layer of sand or pea gravel in the hole, and insert the post (the idea is to keep the concrete from sealing the bottom of the post). Backfill with concrete, and jab it with a shovel handle to remove any air pockets. With a trowel, slope the top of the collar so that water will drain away from the post. Plumb the post with a level.

The fence is installed one of two ways, depending on the design. On some fences, set all of the posts at one time, then attach the panels or rails between them. On other fences, you install a post, a panel, then a post, another panel, and so on. Follow the manufacturer's installation procedures for the style you've chosen.

3 Attaching the Panels. With a helper, fit the panels or rail assemblies between the posts. The rails fit into holes in the posts. The top rail is usually secured with screws, and the lower rails are secured with plastic lock rings or clips, which must

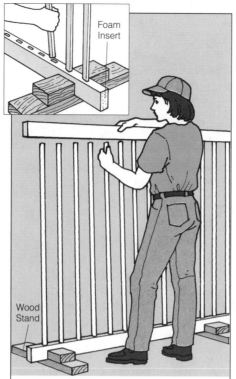

1 Attach the rails to the pickets before the fence is installed. A wood stand helps hold the fence while you work on it.

2 Sand at the bottom of the hole keeps concrete from filling the cavity in the post and allowing water to build up.

Attach rails, then plumb and brace post.

Screw top rail in place.

Plumb and brace post.

3 Install panels before the posthole concrete hardens.

be inserted into the rail ends before they go into the posts.

There's no need to wait for the concrete to set around the posts before you attach the panel. Pour the concrete in a half dozen or so postholes, stick the posts in, and slip the panels between them before the concrete sets up. Then adjust the posts so that they are level and plumb. Hold the posts in position with temporary braces until the concrete hardens.

4 Reinforcing the End and Gate Posts.
Vinyl bends much more easily than metal, so on many designs, the end and gate posts are reinforced with two lengths of ½-inch rebar and mortar. Reinforcing is usually done after the panels are installed and after the concrete in the postholes has cured for about two days. Typically, the rebar is about half the length of the post. After inserting the rebar where shown, make a pourable mortar mix and pour it to the top of the post. (Use a coffee can with the rim bent to form a spout.)

5 Finishing the Fence.
Use post caps to prevent water from accumulating inside. On the design shown, the cap is secured to the post with a small screw. On other designs, you glue the cap on with PVC cement. (Be careful not to get any cement on exposed surfaces.) After the fence is assembled, immediately clean it with water and a plastic scouring pad or soft cloth. Do not use steel wool pads or abrasive cleansers because they will mar the vinyl surface.

6 Dealing with Special Situations.
Some vinyl fence panels can be pushed out of square (racked) to follow a slope. You may have to miter the ends of the rails and pickets, as shown. Ends can be mitered with a back saw and adjustable miter box, a power miter saw equipped with a fine-tooth blade, or by simply marking the angle on the rail end and cutting with a fine-tooth hand saw. If the slope is greater than a 2-inch rise per 12-inch run, the holes in the posts may need to be enlarged to accept the slanted rails. You can enlarge the holes with a straight bit in a router. Guide the cut with the router's fence attachment.

Certain vinyl-fence designs can also be stepped, but you will need longer posts than you would use for a conventional fence. Order end posts, which have holes on one side only, for all of the fence posts that will step down the hill. Rout a pair of holes on the blank side using a template (available from the supplier) to guide a router with a ⅛-inch straight bit. Doing this will allow your fence to be racked to follow a slope.

4 Vinyl bends easily, so reinforce the gate and end posts with rebar and mortar.

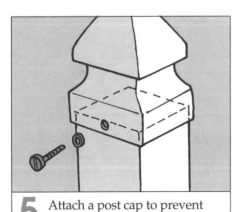

5 Attach a post cap to prevent water from collecting.

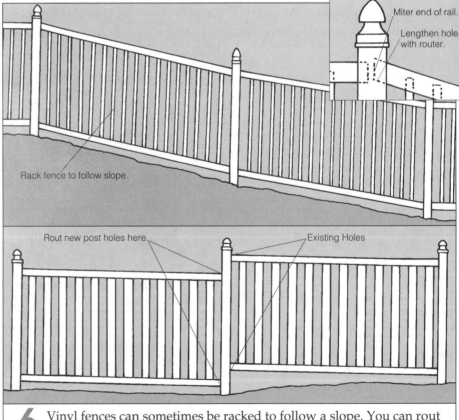

6 Vinyl fences can sometimes be racked to follow a slope. You can rout holes in end posts to create posts for a stepped fence.

Chain Link Fences

Chain link fences are durable and can provide excellent security. Because these fences don't block views, they are a good choice for keeping an eye on pets and small children. Most home centers, lumberyards, and fence suppliers stock all of the parts required, including the chain link mesh, posts, rails, and hardware. Just tell the dealer how long and how tall you want the fence to be. He or she will help you select necessary components to build the fence. Remember to specify whether or not you want to include a chain link gate in the project.

The chart, Chain Link Fence Components, shows the materials required to construct a chain link fence.

Types of Chain Link

Chain link mesh may be galvanized with zinc, or it may be aluminum coated for even more durablility. You can also buy vinyl-coated chain link, usually in white, black, brown, or green. Dark colors generally blend into the surroundings, making the fence less visible. Matching vinyl sleeves are also available to cover the tubular metal posts and rails. Galvanized mesh is usually the least expensive, but durability (and price) depend on the quality of the galvanized coating. Vinyl chain link is the most expensive, but offers more design choices, and generally outlasts galvanized or aluminum mesh. Aluminum is generally better than galvanized because it looks nicer and lasts a bit longer than galvanized mesh.

Chain Link Inserts. When choosing chain link mesh, look at the link top. The wire ends can be either bent over or twisted upward to form barbs. The barbs are good for security but can cause injury. Where privacy is a consideration, you can weave slats of wood, metal, or plastic into the mesh, as shown on the next page. Plastic and metal inserts come in a wide range of colors, which can be mixed and matched to achieve different design effects. The inserts

Chain Link Fence Components

Fence Hardware	Use
Terminal post	Placed at fence ends, corners, and gates
Line post	Placed at intervals between terminal posts on fence
Tension band	Attaches fence to terminal post
Brace band	Slips over terminal post and attaches to rail end
Post cap	Protects top of terminal post
Eye top	Supports top rail; protects top of line post
Top rail	Forms top of fence; helps support chain link mesh
Rail end	Supports rail at terminal post
Top-rail sleeve	Joins sections of top rail. Not necessary if one rail slips into the next.
Tension bar	Holds end of chain link mesh taut against terminal post
Chain link mesh	Attaches to posts and rails to create a durable barrier
Tie wire	Secures chain link mesh to posts and intermediate rails

Gate Hardware	Use
Post hinge	Bolted to gate post; supports swinging gate
Gate hinge	Attached to gate by manufacturer; slips over pin on post hinge
Fork latch	Attached to gate by manufacturer; holds gate shut
Carriage bolt	Variety of sizes supplied by manufacturer for attaching fence and gate components

can be installed either vertically or diagonally. For a more natural look, you can plant tall shrubs against the fence or raise vines on it. Chain link provides sturdy support for heavy vines, such as ivy, wisteria, or honeysuckle.

Building a Chain Link Fence

Chain link fences are not a popular do-it-yourself project. Many people are intimidated by the number of components and because metal is not as user-friendly as wood. Although tall fences are best installed by a fence contractor, low chain link fences (48 inches or less) are actually simple to install. Chain link mesh usually comes in long rolls and must be cut to the right size, which is done simply by snipping the wire with lineman's pliers and undoing the manufactured, wire-strand weave.

In order to properly install a chain link fence, you may need a fence-puller, the tool that stretches the chain link mesh between the posts. A fence-puller consists of a winch (known as a come-along), a chain, and a fence-pulling rod. Fence-pullers are difficult to track down; you may have to check several tool rental shops before you find one that carries fence-pullers.

1 Laying Out and Digging the Postholes. Lay out the fence line and determine posthole locations, as described in Chapter 2 "Setting Posts," page 12. Space the posts no farther than 96 inches apart or as specified in the manufacturer's instructions and local building codes. Terminal (end and corner) postholes are typically 8 inches in diameter, and 18 to 30 inches deep. Holes for line posts are 6 inches in diameter and 18 to 24 inches deep, depending on the fence height and soil conditions. In colder climates, set the posts below the frost line. Check local codes.

2 Setting the Posts. Separate the terminal posts (end, corner, and gate posts) from the line posts (intermediate posts). Terminal posts typically have a larger diameter than line posts. All posts should be set in concrete. Use a fairly stiff mix, and frequently check the posts for plumb with a level. It's necessary to prop the posts with short lengths of lumber until the concrete sets.

Set the terminal posts first. Once the terminal posts are in, attach a leveled string between them marking the height of the line posts. (Line posts are usually about four inches lower than terminal posts because the rails cross over them. Check your manufacturers' specifications.) Set the line posts to this height.

3 Adding the Top Rails. In one or two days, after the concrete

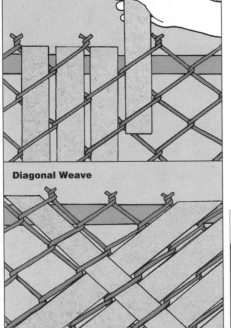

Chain Link Inserts. Wood, aluminum, or vinyl can be woven into the chain link to provide privacy.

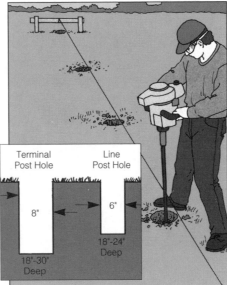

1 Lay out the posts, and dig holes for them no farther than 96 inches apart.

2 Set the terminal posts. Stretch a string between them to mark the height of the line posts.

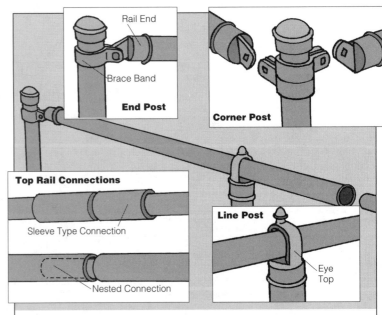

3 After the concrete has cured, attach hardware to the end posts and to the top of the line posts.

has completely set, slide onto each terminal post the tension bands (three or four, depending on fence height), a brace band to anchor the top rail, and a terminal post cap. Gently tap the eye-tops into the ends of the line posts using a hammer and wood block. Bolt the rail ends onto the brace bands on the terminal posts, then install the top rails, slipping them through the eye-top connectors on the line posts and into the rail

ends. Often, one end of each rail is reduced in diameter so that it can be fitted snugly into the rail preceding it. In other cases, rail sleeves may be required to connect rail ends. Rail-to-rail connections do not have to occur exactly above a post, although the installation will be stronger if they do.

4 **Stretching the Chain Link.** With a helper, unroll several feet of chain link mesh and weave a tension

bar into the end of the mesh. Attach the bar to the tension bands on the end or corner post using the carriage bolts provided. Next, unroll the mesh to the other end of the fence, pull the mesh tight by hand, and weave a fence-pulling rod into the mesh about 36 inches in front of the end post. The pulling rod has holes through it which you attach a chain with S-hooks in the ends. Hook one end of a come-along winch to the pulling rod and the other end to the end post. Then crank the come-along to tighten the mesh. Test for tautness by pinching the mesh shut. The fence is taut enough when the openings close no more than about ½ inch. Weave a tension bar into the mesh even with the end post. With lineman's pliers cut the top and bottom links just beyond the tension bar. Undo the wire between the cuts to separate the mesh into two parts. Attach the tension bar to the tension bands with carriage bolts. On short runs of fence with light-weight chain link, a come-along may not be needed. Simply have a helper stretch the mesh by hand as you fasten it to the posts.

5 **Fastening the Chain Link to the Rails.** Attach the chain link mesh to the top rails and line posts with short pieces of galvanized wire or special wire ties, available from the supplier. Hook one end of the tie to

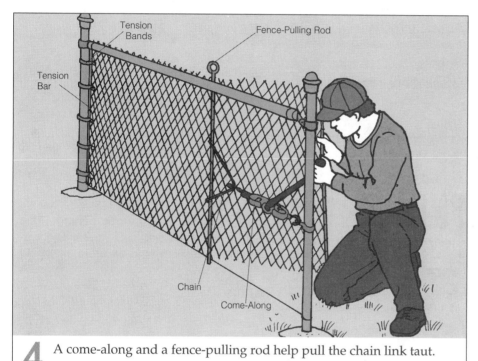

4 A come-along and a fence-pulling rod help pull the chain link taut.

5 The top of the chain link is attached to the fence with metal ties. The bottom often has a cable woven through it that is attached to the posts.

6 Stretch the chain link across the gate frame by hand, and hang the gate with the hardware that comes with it.

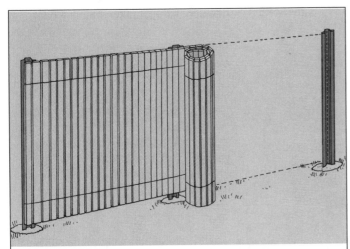

Utility Fencing. Utility fencing, also called snow fencing, consists of narrow wood slats held together with wire.

Wire Picket Fencing. Wire picket fencing comes in rolls or in short, flat lengths. It is simply pushed into the ground.

the mesh, curl the tie over the post or rail, then hook the other end on the mesh. Space ties 24 inches apart on the rails and 12 inches apart on each line post. On some designs, a heavy gauge wire is woven through the chain link mesh at the bottom of the fence. It is attached to the end posts to provide additional stability and to keep the chain link from bowing. Attach the wire to one end post by forming a loop around the post and cinching it with a cable clamp to cinch the wire. Weave the wire through the links about 4 inches above the bottom edge of the mesh, stretch it tight, and attach to the opposite end post.

6 Installing the Gate. Gates usually come with hinges and latch attached. For an extra cost, you can have the gate set up with chain link mesh. If you choose to do it yourself, weave a tension bar in one end of the chain link mesh and attach it to the gate frame with tension bands. Stretch the mesh hand tight, weave a second bar even with the gate frame, cut the mesh just beyond the tension bar, and attach with tension bands. Attach the top and bottom of the mesh to the gate frame with wire ties. Next, determine which side of the gate will be hinged, bolt the hinge pins to the gate post, and hang the gate on the pins. Test the gate and adjust the hinges if necessary. You also may have to adjust

the latch so that it is at a comfortable height; 36 inches is common.

Quick, Easy Fences

Sometimes, you may need to install a temporary fence or screen that can be removed later when plans change or when you build a permanent fence. Other simple designs can be permanent features in the yard.

Utility Fencing. Utility fencing consists of wooden slats wired together. It is sold in large rolls, in heights from 36 to 72 inches. You simply unroll the fencing and nail or wire it to permanent or temporary wood or metal posts. While not especially attractive or durable, utility fencing provides a barrier to keep people and animals out of a designated area. Utility fencing is also called snow fencing because you can place it strategically to prevent snow from drifting across sidewalks or driveways.

Wire Picket Fencing. Wire picket fencing is also sold in rolls at home-and-garden centers and is used as a low temporary or decorative border around planting beds and walks. These welded-wire fences are either factory-painted or vinyl-coated and come in heights from 12 to 18 inches. To install, you simply unroll the wire and stick it into the ground. Low,

prefabricated picket fence sections made of wood or PVC plastic are also available. These, too, are simply pushed into the ground and removed when your landscape plans change.

Reed and Bamboo Screening. Reed and bamboo screening consist of a light reed or split bamboo material woven together with thin wire. Typically, they are sold in 72- or 96-inch widths in rolls 25 or 50 feet long. The lightweight screening can be attached vertically to posts or a wooden frame to provide shade and privacy. It can also be used to dress up the frame side of a board fence. While bamboo and reed screening make attractive, natural-looking backdrops for informal gardens, they quickly deteriorate when exposed to the weather, so you can't expect them to last more than three to five years.

Rope or Chain Fences. Rope or chain fences make attractive, economical boundary markers for large areas, especially along paths, walks, long driveways, or roadsides. To make one, you simply drill holes through low 4x4 or 6x6 posts and thread a length of chain or heavy rope through the holes. At end or corner posts, you attach the rope or chain to the post with large eyescrews. Attach chain by putting an S-hook in the end. Attach rope by making a loop at the end and cinching it with a wire clamp.

BUILDING & INSTALLING GATES

Gates can be simple or ornate, formal or informal, traditional or contemporary, inviting or forbidding. To call attention to an opening, choose a design that contrasts with the surrounding fence or wall. Similarly, you can call attention to the gate by changing the size, spacing, or direction of the siding materials used on the fence. Conversely, you may want a gate that provides a sense of security and privacy. Gates leading to side yards or backyards, for example, can be constructed from the same materials as the fence to lend the impression of an unbroken barrier. Tall, heavy, solid gates send a clear message that the owners value their privacy.

Gate Design & Function

Most gates are made either of wood or ornamental metal. You can choose from a variety of prefabricated designs or create your own. No matter what design you choose, the gate must be sturdy and swing freely without sagging or binding. The most successful wood gates use lightweight, kiln-dried wood and heavy-duty hinges, and have braces to prevent sagging.

Gate Size and Weight. Spacing between gate posts should be from 36 to 48 inches, depending on the gate's function and location. Posts for gates leading to a house's front door should be 48 inches apart, which allows room for two people to pass through at once. Posts for gates leading to backyards or side yards should be spaced no less than 36 inches apart so that lawn mowers, wheelbarrows, and other wheeled garden equipment may fit through the opening.

Even for low gates, you need to set the posts a minimum of 24 inches in the ground, or below the frost line in cold climates. Take extra care to plumb both posts so that they are exactly the same distance apart at the top and bottom.

If you're installing a prefabricated gate, space the posts to provide clearance on the latch side and

hinge side. In most cases, you'll leave ½ inch of clearance on the hinge side and ½ to ¾ inches of clearance on the latch side; but you should use the clearances specified in the gate manufacturer's instructions. The clearances required for chain link and ornamental metal gates are usually determined by the type of hardware used to attach them to posts.

Usually, gates are the same height as the fence or wall, but not necessarily. The gate's height depends on its function, and on the fence design. If a fence or wall provides security and privacy, you'll want to make the gate the same height and as difficult to climb as the wall.

Keep the weight of the gate in mind when choosing materials. The gate should be sturdy enough to stand up to continuous use and abuse, but not so heavy that it's hard to open and close. Large, solid-board gates tend to be heavy and may require three or even four hinges to support them. If the gate swings over a smooth, hard surface, such as a walk, you can install a caster, or wheel, on the bottom of a heavy gate to relieve strain on the hinges and to keep the gate from sagging (see the drawing on page 60).

Selecting the Location. Usually, gates are located where a fence or wall will cross an existing or proposed

Selecting the Location. Place a gate 36 to 48 inches back from a busy sidewalk so that there is a clear place to stand while opening it.

walkway or entry. In a new landscape, these elements are planned simultaneously as part of the overall scheme.

If you are installing a front boundary fence directly next to a sidewalk (especially a busy one), it is good practice to jog the fence back 36 to 48 inches from the sidewalk and install the gate there. Setting the gate back from the sidewalk gives visitors a place to open the gate without having to stand in the middle of the sidewalk.

Direction of Swing. Entry gates traditionally open inward toward the

Direction of Swing. When planning your gate, determine how the direction of swing will affect traffic through the gate. In most cases, a front yard entry gate swings inward, toward the house. Use adjacent walls or fences as places to mount hardware that will keep the gate open.

house. (Your front door swings in the same direction, although there's no hard-and-fast rule about this.) The direction of swing depends largely on the gate location and features on either side of the gate. For example, if the gate crosses a sloping walk, it may have to swing downhill to provide clearance at the bottom of the gate. If a gate is located at the corner of a fence, or at right angles to a wall, or other structure, it is usually best to have the gate swing toward the structure. You can attach a simple hook-and-eye screw to the structure and the gate to keep the gate open when necessary. The direction of swing will also influence the type and mounting location of hinges and latches and vice versa.

Gate Hardware

Hinges and latches range from utilitarian to ornamental. Choose a style that is appropriate for the fence design, and consider whether the hardware will be mounted on the face or edge of the gate. Some gates are designed to look like doors. These gates may call for concealed hinges, in which only the hinge pin is visible. In this case, utilitarian butt hinges will do the job.

Hinges. Hinges come in a wide variety of shapes and sizes, but there are four basic types: butt hinges, T-hinges, strap hinges, and hook-and-strap hinges. When choosing hinges, make sure they are designed for exterior use and are heavy enough to support the weight of the gate. Because most failures in gates result from inadequately sized hinges, choose the heaviest hinges you can install that are still in visual scale with the gate.

Gate Latches. You have many choices when it comes to gate latches. Some of the more popular styles are shown here. Many latches are designed to be fitted with a padlock, or you can install a separate lock and hasp. On seldom-used gates, a hasp alone may suffice. Formal door-

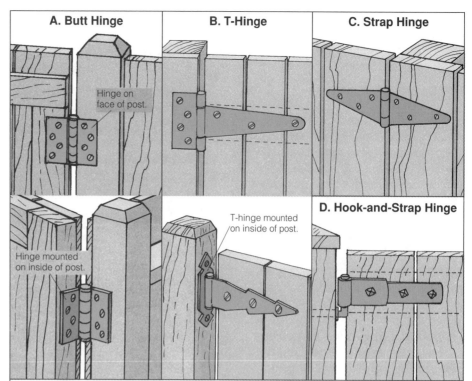

Hinges. Butt hinges (A) have two rectangular leaves joined by a hinge pin. They may be mounted on the outside faces of the post and gate or concealed between the gate frame and post. T-hinges (B) are usually sized by the length of the long hinge leaf. This leaf mounts on the gate surface and can support more weight than a butt hinge. Strap hinges (C) are mounted on the outside faces of the gate and fence, and their long leaves make them even stronger than T-hinges. Hook-and-strap hinges (D) consist of an L-shaped lag screw secured to the post and a leaf or strap fastened to the gate. These strong hinges can be used with square or round posts.

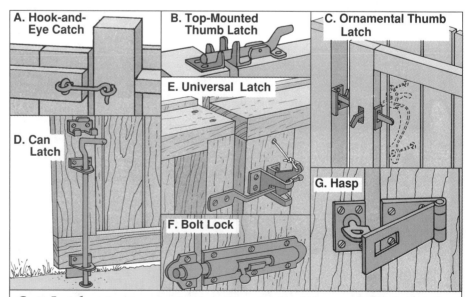

Gate Latches. Inexpensive hook-and-eye latches (A) are suitable for small garden gates. Thumb latches are available in two versions: top-mounted (B) and ornamental (C). Can latches (D) are mounted vertically at the bottom of the gate. Universal gate latches (E) automatically capture the strike bar when you shut the gate. Locks include bolts (F) and hasps (G).

style gates, such as those leading to a courtyard or front-entry enclosure, can employ conventional door locksets or deadbolts.

Other Hardware

On very wide or heavy gates, additional hardware may be required to keep the gate from sagging. Even if the gate you constructed doesn't feel very heavy, fasteners often work themselves loose in time. So it is always a good idea to install anti-sag hardware, which will keep the gate in good working condition for a long time.

Sag Rods. Sag rods or cables with adjustable turnbuckles can be used to keep gates from sagging or binding or to shore up a leaning gate post. The rods are easy to install. They are typically sold as kits that include a pair of threaded rods, a turnbuckle, and fastening hardware. A cable may be substituted for the threaded rods. If a cable is used, hooks in each end of the turnbuckle attach to the gate and to the cable.

On gates, sag rods and cables work by pulling up the sagging end. Install them diagonally with the high end at the top hinge and the bottom of the rod fastened to the bottom corner of the gate, as shown below.

Fence posts are exactly the opposite. On fence posts, attach the rod so that it runs from the upper end of the leaning post to the lower end of its neighbor, as shown.

Casters. Where wide or heavy gates cross a relatively smooth, level surface, such as a walk or driveway, a wheel or caster installed at the bottom front corner of the gate frame effectively prevents sagging. If the siding extends below the frame, you may have to mount the caster on a block, as shown.

Gate Springs. You can make your gate close automatically with the help of a gate spring. A gate spring consists of a long, heavy spring and two brackets or eye screws, usually sold as a kit in hardware stores. One bracket or screw mounts to the gate, the other to the fence with the spring mounted to them. When combined with a self-latching universal gate latch, this combination will pull the gate shut and keep it shut—a good feature if you have pets or small children.

Casters. If a gate is over a paved surface, a heavy-duty rubber caster will support the weight, preventing the gate from sagging.

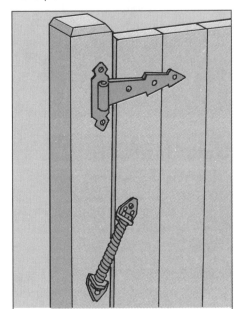

Gate Springs. A spring mounted on the hinge side can pull a gate shut automatically.

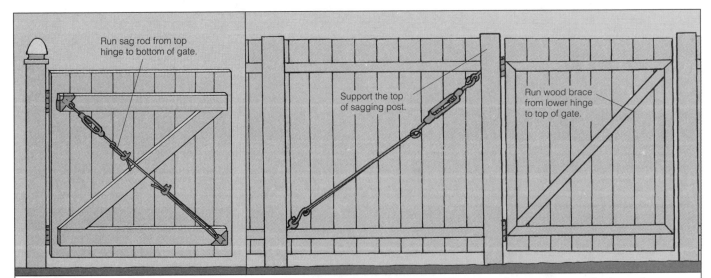

Run sag rod from top hinge to bottom of gate.

Support the top of sagging post.

Run wood brace from lower hinge to top of gate.

Sag Rods. A sag rod or a wooden brace can keep a gate from drooping. The sag rod runs diagonally from the upper hinge to a lower corner. A post brace runs in the opposite direction.

Building a Wooden Gate

Most wooden gates employ a braced frame of 2x4s to which you attach the siding of your choice. But before you start building, it is a good idea to spend some time with the posts that will support the gate.

With a level, double check to make sure the fence posts on either side of your gate opening are plumb. Then measure the distance between posts at both the top and the bottom, and make sure the distance is the same.

If a post is seriously misaligned, either reposition it with a sag rod, or take it out and reset it. Discrepancies of a ½ inch or less probably won't interfere with the gates operation or appearance. In that case, install the gate, and if necessary, correct the sag later.

Making a Gate-on-Frame

This is a simple, sturdy gate, which can be altered to match almost any fence design. To determine the gate width, measure the distance between the gate posts, then subtract 1 to

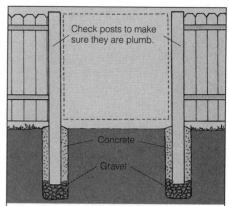

Building a Wooden Gate. Check the gate opening to make sure the gate posts are plumb.

Making a Sliding Latch

This simple sliding latch lends itself well to rustic board fences and gates. It provides good security because it can only be opened from one side of the gate. If you want to operate the latch from both sides, cut a horizontal slot in the gate and extend the dowel handle through the gate. Be sure to provide adequate backing for any loose fence boards.

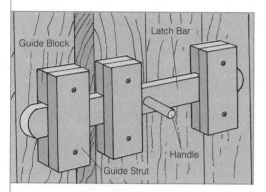

Cutting List

Qty.	Part	Dimensions	Comments
One	Latch Bar	¾" x 1½" x 11¾"	Cut from 1x2
One	Handle	½" dia. dowel x 4"	Cut from ½"-dia. dowel
Three	Guide Struts	¾" x 1½" x 4⅝"	Cut from 1x2
Six	Guide Blocks	¾" x 1½" x 1½"	Cut from 1x2
Six	2-inch Screws		

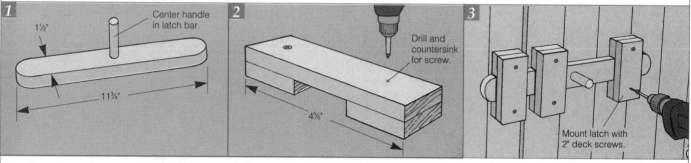

1. Making the Latch Bar. Cut the latch bar to size. Lay out the rounded ends with a compass set to a ¾-inch radius and cut them with a saber saw. Drill a ½-inch diameter hole through the latch for the handle. Cut the dowel to length, and glue it in place with an exterior-grade wood glue.

2. Making the Guide Assemblies. Cut the guide blocks and guide struts to the dimensions in the cutting list. Because the supporting blocks are so small, you may find it easier (and safer) to cut them with a hand saw. Assemble the blocks and struts with construction adhesive. Add a brad in each small support block if you don't want to wait for the adhesive to set.

3. Assembling the Latch. Next, tack the latch bar in level position across the gate with two finishing nails. The

bar (tacked temporarily) will serve as the mounting guide for the blocks and struts. Hold each assembly over the latch bar, and drill two pilot holes about half the diameter of the screw shank as shown. Finish the job by driving screws through the pilot holes into the fence—one top and bottom on each assembly—then pull your tacks to release the latch bar.

1¼ inches to allow clearance for the hinges and latch.

1 Cutting the Gate Frame.

Use straight, kiln-dried lumber for the gate frame. The ends can be either mitered or cut square: Mitered joints look better, but butt joints tend to be a little stronger. For the strongest, best-looking joints, make half-lap joints by notching the rails to accept the stiles. For more on cutting notches, see "Dadoing Posts," page 29.

In most situations, the horizontal frame parts are aligned with the fence rails to maintain the horizontal structural lines inside the fence. Cut the horizontal frame parts to run the entire width of the gate. Cut the vertical parts to a length that allows for your joinery and rail position.

2 Assembling the Gate Frame.

Lay the frame members on a flat work surface, then join them with 10d galvanized nails or 2-inch deck screws to form four square corners. Metal brackets can be used to provide additional strength at joints.

3 Bracing the Frame.

This gate is braced by a 2x4 that runs diagonally from the bottom of the hinge side to the top of the latch side. Lay the 2x4 diagonally under the frame and mark the cut line with a pencil. Cut the brace to fit tightly into the frame corners. Attach by toenailing the brace into the frame corners with 7d galvanized nails or 2-inch deck screws. Predrill nail or screw holes to avoid splitting board ends.

4 Attaching the Fence Boards.

For solid-board designs, leave at least ¼-inch spaces between boards to allow for expansion during humid weather. Mark the board locations and spacing on the face of the frame, and use galvanized nails or deck screws to attach the boards to the frame and diagonal brace. On some gates, the siding on the latch side extends past the frame to serve as a gate strike (see next step). Frequently check that

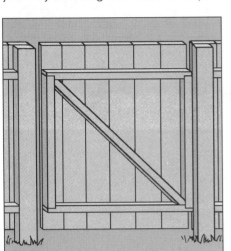

Making a Gate-on-Frame. The most basic gate is a frame and a brace with fence boards nailed to it. It is strong and versatile enough to match almost any fence.

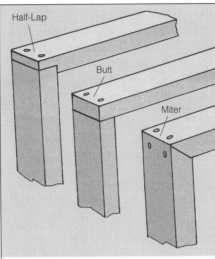

1 You can make the gate with any of a variety of reinforced joints. The half-lap is the strongest, followed by the butt, and then the miter joint.

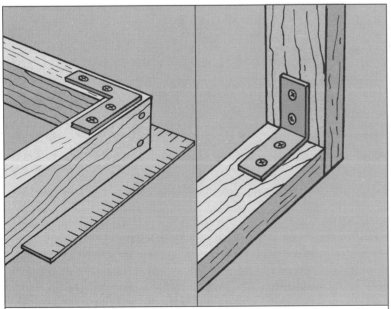

2 Check to make sure the frame is square, and reinforce it with metal brackets.

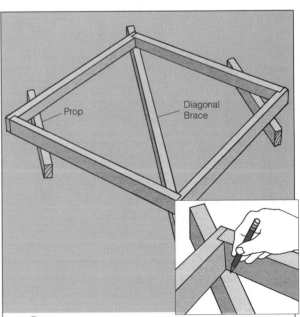

3 Mark the length of the brace and the angle at the ends by placing the brace under the frame and tracing with a pencil.

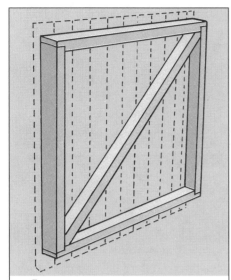

4 Attach the boards to the frame. Check often to be sure the frame has remained square.

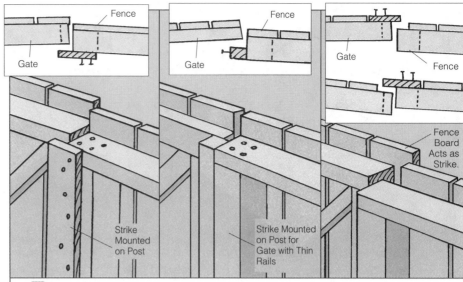

5 A gate strike keeps the gate from swinging past the opening when you close it. You can attach the strike to either side of the fence and to either the post or the gate.

Fence

Gate

Fence

Gate

Gate

Fence

Fence Board Acts as Strike.

Strike Mounted on Post

Strike Mounted on Post for Gate with Thin Rails

the frame remains square during assembly and that the fence boards are perpendicular to the rails.

5 **Attaching the Gate Strike.** A gate strike keeps the gate from swinging past its closure point and bending the hinges. (Some gate latches, such as the universal latch shown on page 59, can serve as a gate strike.) You'll need to install a strike board on the gate or the gate post. The location of the strike depends on gate design and the direction the gate opens. Design also dictates whether you install the strike before or after you hang the gate. Use galvanized fasteners.

Making a Z-Brace Gate

This simple gate, reminiscent of rustic batten doors found on barns and other outbuildings, is easy to make and uses a minimum of lumber. Typically, a Z-brace gate is found on a solid-board fence, a masonry wall, or a breezeway between buildings.

The design shown uses 1x8 fence boards with dog-eared tops. Boards ranging from 1x4 to 1x10 would also work. If you want a narrower gate, use 1x6 instead of 2x4 for the braces.

1 **Laying Out the Fence Boards.** Measure the opening and determine how many boards you will need.

Allow for ¼-inch spaces between the boards. If necessary, rip boards to width. If possible, rip the two outside pieces so that you don't have a single skinny piece of one side of the gate.

Cut the dog ears. Lay the boards in position on a flat surface. Use scraps of ¼-inch plywood for spacers and make sure the gate is square.

2 **Installing the Horizontal Braces.** Cut the 2x4 horizontal braces to be as long as the gate is wide. Position them on the siding so they will match the fence rails. If you are attaching the gate to masonry or a fence that has no visible rails, position

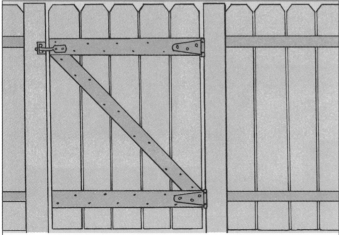

Making a Z-brace Gate. A Z-brace gate is simple to build. Use T-hinges to fasten the gate to the fence post.

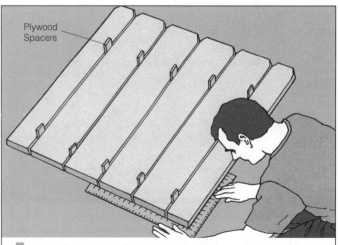

Plywood Spacers

1 A Z-brace gate begins with the boards. Lay them on a flat surface and space them evenly.

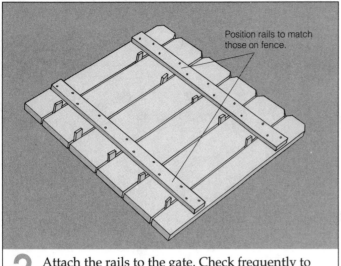

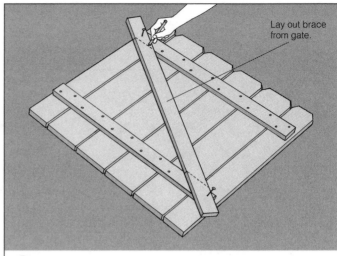

2 Attach the rails to the gate. Check frequently to make sure they stay aligned and correctly spaced.

3 Place wood for the brace on the gate, and mark the length of the brace and the angles of the end cuts.

the braces 8 inches from the top and bottom of the gate. Attach them by driving two 2-inch galvanized deck screws into each board. Stagger the screws as shown. Remove the plywood spacers.

3 Installing the Angled Brace. To measure for the angled brace, place a 2x4 in position on top of the horizontal braces, and mark it for the cuts. Install by driving two 2-inch screws into each fencing board. Stagger the screws so that they do not follow along a grain line

in the brace—otherwise, the brace may split.

Making a Diagonal-Board Gate

Placing boards on an angle gives a gate extra strength. In this design, 1x8 tongue-and-groove cedar siding is sandwiched diagonally between two 1x6 frames, creating a solid entry gate that looks the same on both sides. A 2x3 cap rail protects the end grain of the siding pieces from the weather.

This design lends itself well to double gates. Hang the gates so the diag-

onals of each gate run in opposite directions, creating a herringbone effect. For maximum strength, be sure the diagonal pattern runs from the top of the latch side to the bottom of the hinge side.

1 Cutting the Frames. Cut four pieces of 1x6 to the height of the gate, and four pieces to the width, minus 11 inches, to take into account the width of two pieces of 1x6.

Lay the pieces in place, as shown, on a flat surface. Make sure the unit

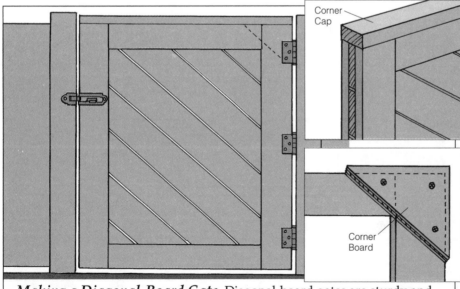

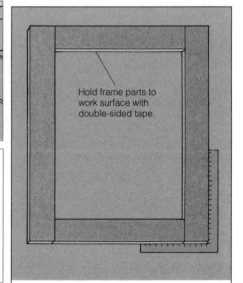

Making a Diagonal-Board Gate. Diagonal-board gates are sturdy and attractive, and may not require additional anti-sag bracing. On double gates, alternate the direction of diagonal boards on each section to make a herringbone pattern.

1 Put double-sided carpet tape on the frame parts, and lay them on a clean work surface, making sure the assembly is square.

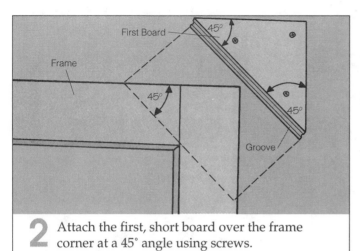

2 Attach the first, short board over the frame corner at a 45° angle using screws.

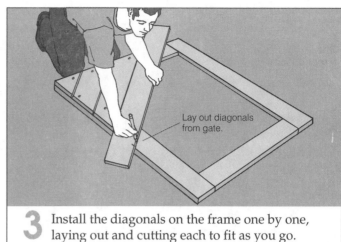

3 Install the diagonals on the frame one by one, laying out and cutting each to fit as you go.

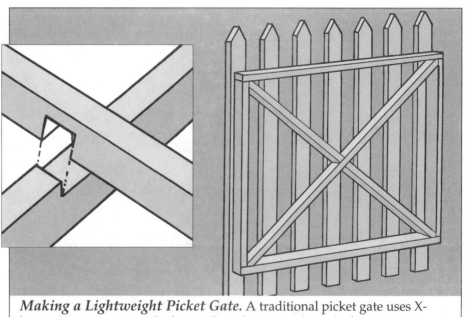

4 Once all the diagonals are installed, attach the outer frame and the cap rail.

is square. If possible, anchor the pieces in place to make construction of the gate easier. You can anchor them by taping them to a plywood work surface with double-sided carpet tape. If you don't anchor the pieces, periodically make sure they are square.

2 Cutting and Installing the First Diagonal. Cut a right-angle triangle from a piece of 1x6 tongue-and-groove siding, so the groove is along the longest side of the triangle. You can do this by making two 45-degree cuts, as shown.

Fasten this piece to the top of the side that the hinges will go on, so that the two shorter sides are flush with the edges of the frame. (If the hinges will go on the left, the piece will go in the upper left-hand corner.) Drill pilot holes to avoid splitting this small

piece, and drive three 1¼-inch galvanized deck screws through the triangle and into the 1x6 frame.

3 Cutting and Installing the Rest of the Diagonals. Fit another piece of siding against the first piece, and trace along the gate frame to mark it for cutting. Cut and attach to the frame, driving one 1¼-inch screw at each end. Repeat the procedure for all the other pieces.

4 Installing Other Frame Pieces and Cap Rail. Attach the second set of 1x6s to the opposite side of the gate with 2-inch galvanized deck screws. Drive one into each piece of siding in an alternating pattern, as shown.

Cut a piece of 2x3 cap rail the width of the gate. Install it on the top of the gate, so it hangs over the same amount on each side. Drill pilot holes, and drive 3-inch galvanized deck screws every 6 inches in an alternating pattern so that the rail is attached to the framing pieces on either side.

Making a Lightweight Picket Gate

This gate is lightweight, gaining strength from joinery rather than mass. It will blend in with your picket fence, or it can be used as a decorative feature in its own right. Use 1x3s or 1x4s for the pickets. For variations in the designs of the tops of the pickets, see "Picket-Top Designs," page 38.

Making a Lightweight Picket Gate. A traditional picket gate uses X-bracing to create a sturdy frame. Cut a lap joint where the braces cross.

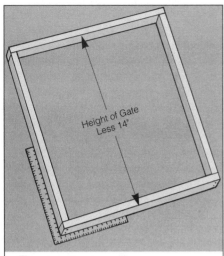

Height of Gate Less 14"

1 Cut the frame parts to size and assemble with butt joints and screws.

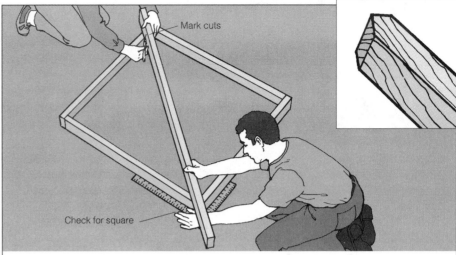

Mark cuts

Check for square

2 Lay out the length of the diagonal and its end angles by placing an oversized brace on the gate and tracing along the frame.

1 **Constructing the Rectangular Frame.** Cut two pieces of 2x3 to the exact width of your gate, and two pieces that are 14 inches shorter than the picket height. On a flat surface, construct a simple box. Drill pilot holes and drive two 3-inch galvanized deck screws through each joint. Make sure the frame is square.

2 **Cutting the Cross Braces.** Set a piece of 2x3 at a diagonal on top of the frame. Mark each end for a pointed cut, so that the piece will fit snugly inside the box. Repeat the

process for a diagonal crosspiece going in the other direction.

3 **Cutting the Half-Lap Joint.** Cut a notch in each brace at the point where they meet so that they fit together. Slip one of the cross braces into position in the frame. Place the second brace in position on top of the first, and mark each to show where they meet.

Take the braces out and place them on a good surface for cutting. Set your circular saw to cut exactly halfway through the width of a 2x3—make

some practice cuts first. For each board, cut to the inside of the two pencil lines. The distance between the two cuts will be 1½ inches, exactly the thickness of a 2x3. Then make a series of closely spaced cuts between the first two cuts. Knock out the waste, and pare the bottom of the notch clean with a chisel.

4 **Attaching the Braces.** Slide the two brace pieces in position. They will fit snugly together. Attach them to the frame by drilling pilot holes and driving 3-inch galvanized deck screws at angles through the

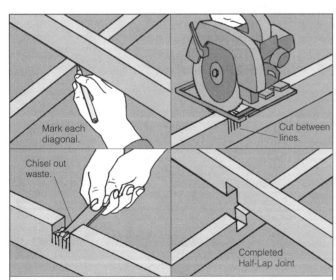

Mark each diagonal.

Cut between lines.

Chisel out waste.

Completed Half-Lap Joint

3 The two parts of a half-lap slip over each other. Lay the boards on top of each other to mark the width of the cut.

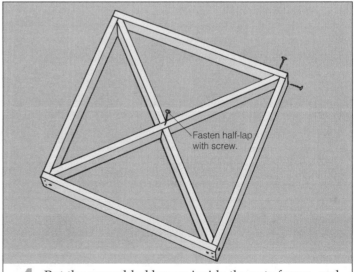

Fasten half-lap with screw.

4 Put the assembled braces inside the gate frame, and screw them in place.

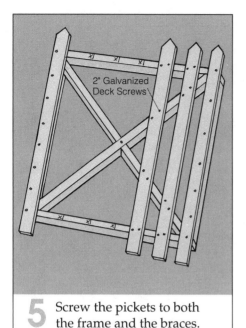

2" Galvanized
Deck Screws

5 Screw the pickets to both the frame and the braces.

frame pieces and into the braces. At the half-lap joint, predrill and drive a 2-inch screw.

5 **Installing the Pickets.** Attach one picket on either end of the gate, flush to the outside edges of the frame. Drill pilot holes, and drive 2-inch screws at 6-inch intervals.

Lay out the remaining pickets so that they will be consistently spaced. The spacing will probably differ from that of the fence. Drill pilot holes, and attach the pickets with two 2-inch screws in the upper rail, lower rail, and cross braces.

Making a Lattice-and-Board Gate

Lattice-and-board fences and gates combine the open, airy feel of lattice with the security and privacy of a solid panel. This gate can be adapted to match an existing fence, or it can provide a pleasing contrast to a solid-board fence.

Because it combines two styles, this gate will take longer to build than other gates. However, no special skills or tools are required. The lattice section may get handled a good deal, so purchase a piece of the good stuff— $\frac{3}{4}$ inch total thickness.

This is a heavy gate, so purchase strong hinges. If you want to make it lighter, use 2x3 instead of 2x4, or purchase light lumber, such as kiln-dried redwood or cedar.

1 **Building a Frame.** Cut two pieces of 2x4 to the width of the gate. Then cut one piece to the width minus 3 inches, and two pieces to the height minus 3 inches. Lay the boards on a flat surface, and put them together as shown, spacing the rails to allow a 12-inch high area for the lattice section. Join the pieces together by drilling pilot holes and driving 3-inch galvanized deck screws.

2 **Attaching the Cleats.** The cleats will hold the lattice and boards in place on the finished fence. Cut pieces of 1x1 to fit snugly between the parts of the frame. Lay scrap pieces of $\frac{5}{8}$-inch plywood down on the flat surface, and use them as spacers to keep the cleats a uniform $\frac{5}{8}$ inch from the edge of the 2x4s. Attach with 4d galvanized finish nails.

3 **Installing the Lattice Panel and the Boards.** Cut a section of a lattice panel to fit, but not snugly. Set it in place on top of the 1x1 cleats, but do not nail it in place. A second set of cleats nailed to the frame will hold the lattice panel in place.

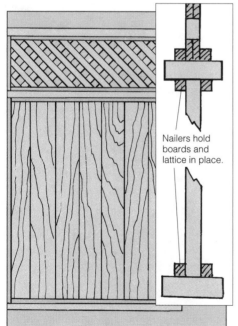

Nailers hold boards and lattice in place.

Making a Lattice-and-Board Gate. This gate uses boards and lattice sandwiched between cleats, as shown.

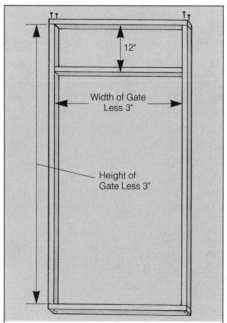

12"

Width of Gate Less 3"

Height of Gate Less 3"

1 Cut the parts and screw the frame together. The short horizontal piece helps hold the lattice in position.

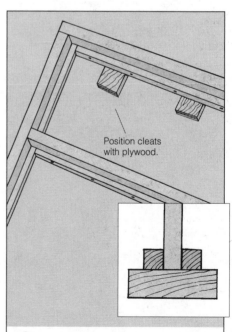

Position cleats with plywood.

2 Nail cleats in place to support the gate boards and lattice. Place scraps of $\frac{5}{8}$-in. plywood under the gate to help position the cleats.

Cut 1x6 boards to fit—again, not snugly—in the lower section of the gate. Set them in place, but do not fasten them.

4 Adding the Second Set of Cleats. Cut pieces of 1x1 to fit snugly, as with the first set of cleats. Push them into position so that they hold the lattice and the 1x6s fairly tightly. Attach them to the 2x4 frame only with 4d galvanized finish nails. Make sure to not attach them to the lattice or the 1x6.

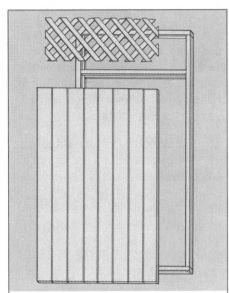

3 Place the lattice and fence boards on top of the cleats, but do not nail them in place.

4 A second set of cleats holds the lattice and fence boards in place. Nail them to the frame but not to the board or lattice.

Hanging a Gate

Whether you are hanging a custom or a prefab gate, you'll need a drill, some wood blocks, and some shims. Although it is possible for one person to do the job, it is always better to have a helper to hold the gate in position and keep it plumb while you attach the hardware.

1 Positioning the Gate. Shim the gate to the right height with wood spacer blocks. Use wood shingle shims, if needed, to get exactly the right height. Use shims or wood strips to space the gate the required clearance from the gate posts. If you're hanging the gate by yourself, you can tack 1x4 cleats to the gate post and temporarily nail the gate to the cleats with 6d nails to make hinge installation easier. Otherwise, have a helper hold the gate in position while you attach the hinges.

2 Attaching the Hinges. Generally, butt hinges are installed about 4 to 6 inches from the top and bottom of the gate. T-hinges and strap hinges usually are installed at the top and bottom rails to provide additional backing for screws. With the gate propped in position, screw or bolt the hinges to the gate post first, according to instructions. Then attach the hinges to the gate. Screws should penetrate as far into the wood as possible without coming out the other side. Predrill all screw or bolt holes to make attachment easier and to avoid splitting the wood. Recheck the position of the gate and adjust, if necessary. Make sure the gate swings freely. If it does not, remove it and trim the bottom as necessary.

3 Attaching the Latch. Attach the gate latch about 36 inches from the ground or according to instructions. In most cases you attach the latch mechanism to the gate first, and then align and attach the strike to the fence. As with hinges, use the longest screws possible. Predrill screw holes.

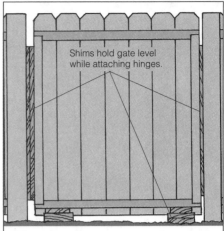

Shims hold gate level while attaching hinges.

1 Put the gate in the opening and shim it with scrap wood to hold the position.

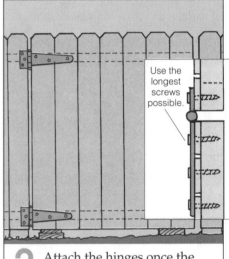

Use the longest screws possible.

2 Attach the hinges once the gate is in place.

3 Attach the latch to the gate first, and then use it to position the strike.

MAINTAINING & REPAIRING FENCES

A well-built fence will last years with a minimum amount of repair. But wind, rain, and weather do take their toll. Your best defense is a good finish. No matter how good the finish, however, be prepared to do some maintenance. The finish will need to be periodically reapplied. Unless your project is built entirely of pressure-treated wood, you should check it once a year for rot and insect damage. And no matter what construction materials you've used to build the fence, be prepared for the occasional repair.

Choosing a Finish

In most cases, people choose a finish based on how they want a fence to look. A redwood or cedar fence probably looks best with a clear finish. A picket fence, on the other hand, traditionally gets a coat of white paint.

But a finish does more than dress up your project. It provides a barrier against the weather. A good finish sheds water, discouraging decay. It seals the wood from the dirt, pollen, and pollution that cause it to turn gray. And because a good finish slows the expansion and contraction of wood caused by changes in humidity, checking and warping are minimized.

There is a wide variety of finishes to choose from, but all fall into one of four basic types.

Water Sealer. Water sealers are typically a wax dissolved in mineral spirits. The wax lodges in the pores of the wood, sealing it against water. The finish is clear, but like all finishes, will darken the color of the wood slightly.

Manufacturers of pressure-treated wood recommend a coat of water sealer once a year. Water sealers are generally applied to all above-ground parts when the project is built. Because the wax wears or is washed away, sealers are reapplied annually to maintain an even, natural wood color. Unfortunately, there are no products on the market that will preserve the color of freshly milled wood—all wood will eventually turn gray or brownish gray.

Stain. Taken by itself, stain does nothing more than color the wood. But some stains have been formulated to provide protection as well. Generally sold as "exterior" or "deck" stains, these are transparent, opaque, or somewhere in between.

Transparent stains are mixed with a preservative. Opaque stains offer more protection than transparent ones because their formula is closer to that of paint. Some inferior brands of stain may not be as durable as paint, but stains do not crack or peel as paint does. Better yet, when it comes time to apply fresh stain in a few years, you won't have to scrape and brush off the old finish. Read the label to make sure the stain is for exterior use and provides protection against mildew and UV rays.

Varnish. In all likelihood you won't be varnishing your fence. Varnish is a combination of an oil and a resin. It is extremely durable, though prone to cracking and flaking. Polyurethane resin varnishes dominate the market these days. Polyurethane is the toughest of the varnishes but not the best for exterior use. Direct sunlight can cause polyurethane to peel, and repairs are almost impossible. Aside from spar varnish, these finishes are best used indoors.

If you're going to use a varnish on a small or specialty fence, choose a spar or marine alkyd resin varnish. Spar and marine vanishes have more oil than other finishes, creating a finish that moves with the wide range of expansion and contraction in wood used outdoors.

Paint. Paint is the most durable of the exterior finishes. It is an excellent wood preservative because it forms a surface film that seals the wood against moisture penetration. You have two choices in exterior paints: acrylic latex or oil. Latex cleans up with soap and water. Oil paints require paint thinner.

At one time, oil was considered much more durable than latex. But formulas have changed over time, and manufacturers now say a top-quality latex paint will hold up just as long as, if not longer than, oil. Both types come in flat, semigloss (satin) and gloss. Better exterior paints also include mildewcides that inhibit the growth of mold, mildew, and decay-causing organisms. Read the label to see what is in the paint you're considering for an exterior finish.

Caution: *Some paints made before 1978 contain lead, which can be hazardous to your health if you try to remove the paint. Environmental laws are strict concerning the disposal of paint debris. If you suspect that a lead-based paint has been used, test it with an inexpensive lead-testing kit available at paint stores. Do not attempt to sand off or otherwise remove lead paint yourself. Hire a professional painting contractor to prepare the fence for repainting.*

Finishing Pressure-Treated Wood

Pressure treating protects wood from insects and rot and is the best thing to use for parts that will come in contact with the ground. It does not prevent checking, cupping or warping, however, so you should protect the wood with a finish. Unfortunately, pressure-treated wood presents some finishing problems. Although the wood has been kiln-dried before treatment, pressure treatment puts water back into the wood, often leaving a water-logged surface that won't hold a finish. Don't apply a finish to any obviously wet wood. Before you apply a finish to pressure-treated wood, test it by sprinkling a few drops of water. If the wood absorbs the water, it is ready to finish. If not, wait. Air circulation will dry out the moisture.

Semitransparent oil-based stains work best on pressure-treated wood. In addition, you should coat the wood annually with water sealer. Manufacturers advise against painting pressure-treated wood with latex.

Application Techniques

Any finish or preservative can be applied by brush, roller, or spray gun. While brushing is the most time-consuming, it is often the best method for painting or staining fences with spaced boards or pickets. Rollers work well for fences with solid-board or plywood siding, but you'll still need a brush to catch areas that the roller doesn't get to.

Application Techniques. Spray guns, at the top, can cover a large surface in a hurry, but make sure you cover adjacent plants and surfaces to protect them from overspray. Brushes make economical use of paint when working on short sections of fence. Keep a brush on hand for touching up spots that rollers or spray guns miss. Rollers work well for flat surfaces. Rather than using a paint tray, buy a clip-on screen that fits into a 2-gallon paint bucket, as shown.

Spray guns work well for designs that would be time consuming to paint with a brush and roller, such as those with latticework or basket weave. A spray gun will not save much time when painting an open design, such as a post-and-rail fence, and you'll end up wasting more paint than you would with a brush and roller. You'll also need to spread drop cloths to prevent overspray from getting on plants, adjacent buildings, patios, and other surrounding surfaces. So even though paint application is often

much quicker with a spray gun, preparation and cleanup time takes much longer. If you have only a short section of fence to paint, it is probably fastest to use a brush or roller.

Redwood and red cedar can be stained or left to weather naturally. Many people actually paint these woods, especially if they're using a cheaper grade wood. Both species "bleed"; that is, the brownish-red tannins in the wood will seep through light-colored paints, discoloring

them. To prevent bleeding on freshly milled redwood or cedar, apply two coats of an oil-based, stain-blocking primer. (Latex stain blockers do not stop stains as well as oil.) A regular primer barely blocks stains at all. Have your paint dealer recommend a blocker that meets your needs.

If bleeding is not a concern, apply an oil or latex primer to all sides of any bare wood. To repaint previously painted fences, remove any peeling or flaking paint with a scraper or putty knife. If the surface is in bad condition, old paint can be removed with a heat gun and putty knife or with a power sander. In both cases, wear a vapor respirator rated to avoid inhaling fumes or dust. Before repainting, scrub the surface with a solution of 1 pound trisodium phosphate (TSP) dissolved in 2 gallons of hot water. This treatment not only removes dirt, grime, and chalking paint; it also softens the old finish to provide better "tooth" for the new paint to stick to. Rinse the fence thoroughly after applying TSP.

Maintaining a Fence

Other than the effects of weather, outdoor structures can be subjected to physical forces, such as frost heave, unstable soil, wind action, and young climbers, all of which can cause a project to sink or lean.

The best way to keep your fence in tip-top shape is to check for damage at least once a year. Add this chore to your spring garden cleanup list.

1 **Checking for Rot.** If your posts are set in gravel, dig around each post to a depth of about 4 inches. Check for decay, probing with an ice pick, knife, or other sharp object. Also check joints where rails meet posts, and where boards attach to rails. Check exposed ends, such as tops of posts and picket boards. If the tool sinks easily into the wood, the wood will have to be repaired or replaced. If decay is less than about ¼ inch deep into the surface, use a paint scraper or wide wood chisel to

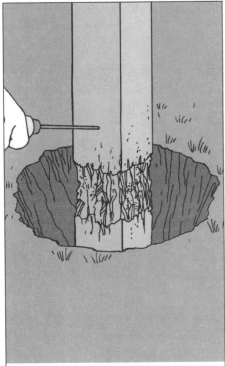

scrape out the decayed area down to sound wood, and then treat with several coats of a good wood preservative or water sealer.

Dry rot is caused by fungi that attacks wood under moist conditions, leaving a dry powdery texture after the wood has dried out. Once the source of moisture is removed, no further decay will occur. Boards with small decayed areas can be scraped to remove the damaged portion and painted or treated with a preservative to prevent future decay.

2 Checking Post Alignment. Use a level to be sure posts are plumb and rails are square to the posts. Minor out-of-square conditions are normal. However, if the fence is dramatically leaning or out of square, consider correcting the condition before it gets any worse.

Grasp the fence near the top, and try to rock it back and forth. If the posts are loose, you should reset them. See if the panels have worked loose. You

can add new posts or rails to shore up dramatically sagging panels.

3 Renailing Loose Rails and Siding. If any of the rails or siding boards have worked loose, renail them. First, try to reset the original nails with a hammer and nail set. Provide additional strength with galvanized deck screws, which are less likely to pop out. Predrill to avoid splitting the wood. If this doesn't provide enough reinforcement, you'll need to add braces to the rails or replace the damaged rails or boards. If you're growing vines against the fence, make sure shoots or tendrils have not worked anything loose. Heavy vines may also cause the fence to lean. Keeping vines neatly trimmed will minimize such damage.

4 Cleaning the Fence. If you'd like to restore that new look to an unfinished fence, apply one of the deck or fence cleaners available at the hardware store. It will remove dirt, mildew, and algae stains, and restore most of the old color to the surface.

1 Check for rot by probing with an ice pick or knife. Decay less than ¼ inch deep can be scraped away. Deeper rot requires more significant repair.

2 Weather or settling may have caused the posts to shift. Make sure they are plumb and that rails are square to them.

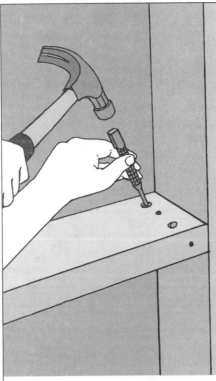

3 Using a hammer, drive loose nails back into the post with a nail set.

4 Wash and scrub the fence to keep it clean. Dirt and mildew may require a commercial deck- or fence-cleaning mixture.

If the fence has been painted or stained, it will still benefit from an occasional cleaning. During the summer, spray down the fence with a strong jet of clear water every few weeks to prevent dirt buildup. If you can't hose the dirt off the fence, rent a pressure washer and clean the fence with a mild detergent. To remove mold and mildew, mix a solution of 1 part chlorine bleach to 10 parts water and apply with a stiff bristle brush. Rinse thoroughly. On painted and stained fences, test these solutions on a small area before doing the entire fence.

Repairing a Fence

Some basic, relatively inexpensive repairs can extend the life of an old fence considerably. If the fence is too far gone, however, you may be better off tearing it down and replacing it. If you do decide to make repairs, consider not only the cost of materials and labor, but also how the fence will look once the repairs are made. Most fence repairs involve repairing or replacing one or more damaged posts. If only a few posts are rotted, and the rest are in good shape, it is worthwhile to replace the damaged ones. If most or all of the posts show damage, you may need to remove the siding and rebuild the entire fence frame. If the siding is still in good shape, you may be able to salvage it for the new fence or use the lumber for other garden projects.

Repairing Damaged Posts

If the post is rotted at or below ground level, but the aboveground portion is still good, you may be able to install a brace instead of replacing it entirely.

1 **Removing Damaged Portions of Posts.** Dig around the existing post down to the bottom. If the post has a concrete collar, break up the concrete with a pick or heavy pry bar and remove the pieces. If the concrete is difficult to remove, consider renting a hammer drill or rotary hammer to break the concrete. Cut off the damaged post about 1 to

2 inches above ground level and remove the rotted portion. When installed, the brace will be in the ground, directly behind the location of the original post. If necessary, widen the hole to accept the brace.

2 **Attaching the Brace.** Cut a brace from a pressure-treated 4x4 to the length shown on the drawing. Bevel the top end to facilitate water runoff. Put the post in the hole, and attach the brace to the post with long carriage bolts. If your fence design won't accommodate this type

of brace or if you simply don't like the looks of it, you can attach pressure-treated 2x4 braces on each side of the post, as shown.

3 **Setting the Brace.** Align the post with the rest of the fence. Plumb the post with a level, and then add a temporary 2x4 brace to keep the post aligned. Set the brace in gravel and concrete, as you would a normal fence post. The concrete collar should extend about 1 inch above ground level and slope away from the post to allow water runoff.

1 To remove a rotten post, first dig around it, then cut off the rotted portion. If there is a concrete collar, break it up and remove it.

2 Cut a single 4x4 brace or two 2x4 braces to replace the rotted section.

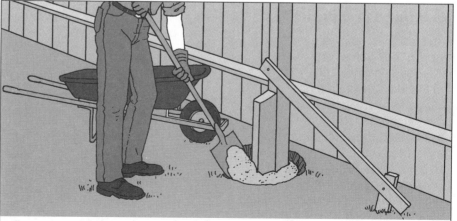

3 Plumb and level the post and set the brace or braces in concrete or gravel.

Replacing Posts

Braces may be aesthetically out of place in some fence designs. If so or if the post is damaged above ground level, replace the entire post.

1 Disconnecting Rails and Siding. Remove the nails connecting the rails and siding boards to the post. A nail puller or small pry bar will give you better leverage and may work better than a hammer. Whatever you use, protect the fence by slipping a piece of wood between it and the nail puller. If necessary, prop up the top rails to keep the fence from sagging while you make repairs.

2 Removing the Damaged Post. If the post is set in earth, use a pry bar to lever the post out of the ground, as shown. If the post is set in concrete, dig around the collar to the bottom, and use a pick or pry bar to break up and remove the concrete. Then pull or pry the post out of the hole. Be sure to remove all rotted wood pieces from the hole because these can attract termites.

3 Adding a New Post. Dig deeper, if necessary, so that the hole is at least 30 inches deep. Put 6 inches of gravel in the hole. Place the new post in the hole, and slip it between the rails. Plumb and brace the post, if necessary, to keep it plumb. Fill the hole with concrete. After the concrete sets, reattach the rails and siding to the new post with galvanized nails or deck screws.

Resetting a Leaning Post

If one or more posts are leaning or loose in their holes, you'll need to reset each one individually to bring the fence back into plumb. To do this, you'll need a tool called a come-along, which is the same device used to stretch chain link fence. (See page 55.) These can be rented at tool rental firms or purchased at a reasonable cost at home centers and hardware stores.

1 To replace a post, first disconnect the rails and siding from it. Slip a piece of scrap between the nail puller and the fence to avoid marring the wood.

2 Remove the post from the ground, breaking up the concrete collar if there is one. To avoid termites, be sure to remove all rotton wood from the hole.

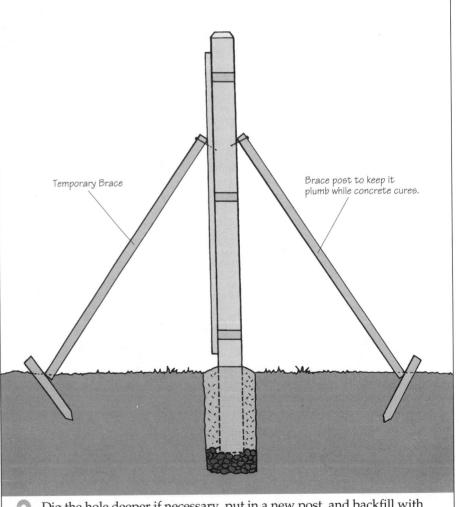

Temporary Brace

Brace post to keep it plumb while concrete cures.

3 Dig the hole deeper if necessary, put in a new post, and backfill with 6 inches of gravel and concrete.

1 To pull a post back into alignment, attach one end of a come-along to the top of the post and the other end to a 36-inch length of ½-inch pipe driven into the ground.

2 When the post is plumb, brace it and fill the hole with gravel and concrete.

1 Pulling the Post into Alignment.
Dig around the post down to the bottom. If the post is set in concrete, break it up with a pick or pry bar and remove the pieces. It is usually not necessary to detach the rails and siding from the post. Attach one end of the come-along to the top of the post, as shown, and the other end to a 36-inch length of ½-inch pipe driven into the ground. Crank the handle on the come-along to bring the post back into alignment. Check the post frequently with a level while operating the come-along.

2 Resetting the Post. Once the post is plumb, secure it with temporary 2x4 diagonal braces, and then backfill the hole with gravel and concrete. Tamp firmly and slope the surface away from the post to divert rain. Once the first post is braced, repeat the procedure for other posts. Allow the concrete to cure (one to two days) before removing the brace.

Repairing Rails & Siding

As a rule, the bottom rails are more prone to decay because they are subjected to more moisture. Be sure to check the rail ends, which usually rot first. By spotting decay early, you can make simple repairs before it is necessary to replace the entire fence. A brace or mending plate is usually enough to reinforce the rail. If damage is severe, you'll need to replace the entire rail: Disconnect it from the post and siding boards; then add a new pressure-treated rail.

Repairing Rails & Siding. Damaged rails can be beefed up by installing a wood support block (left) or a metal T-plate (right). If too much of the rail end is rotted, you'll need to replace the rail.

1 If the hinge screws are loose, fill the holes with epoxy and match sticks or move the hinge to a slightly different location.

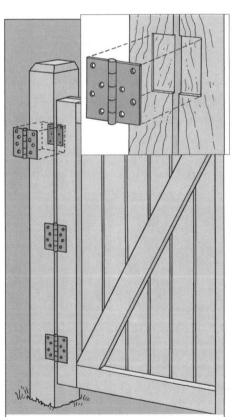

2 If the hinges are bent, replace them with larger hinges and consider adding a third one to help distribute the weight.

Fixing a Sagging Gate

Gates can sag or bind for a variety of reasons: leaning posts, a racked or out-of-square gate frame, loose or bent hinges, or a combination of any of the above. There are several ways to fix these problems.

Loose hinges are one of the most common causes of gate failure, especially if the gate sees heavy use. If the hinges have served the gate for a long time and are still in good shape, the screws may have just worked themselves loose over the years. However, premature hinge failure may be due to hinges that are too small or screws that are too short. You can take the following steps to beef up the hinges.

1 **Tightening Loose Screws.** If the screws are loose, retighten them. If the screw holes are worn to the point that the screws no longer have a good bite, replace the screws with longer ones. If longer screws aren't feasible, epoxy small dowels or wooden match sticks into the old screw holes. When the epoxy dries, predrill new holes, and reattach the hinges. If necessary, you can remove the hinges and relocate them slightly above or below their original position on the gate and post so that you'll be fastening to new wood.

2 **Using Larger or More Hinges.** Loose screws may also indicate that the hinges are too small. Bent hinges are a sure sign of this. Replace them with the largest size that will fit the gate frame and use the longest screws possible. If the gate has only two hinges, add a third hinge halfway between them. Mortising the hinges into the post and gate provides even more strength.

Fixing a Leaning Post

A leaning gate post on the hinge side may be the cause of a sagging gate. If the post leans on the latch side, the gate may bind or the latch won't align properly with the latch strike.

Fixing a Leaning Post. To bring a leaning hinge post back into plumb, connect a sag rod to the top end of the hinge post and the bottom end of the line post, as shown. Tighten the turnbuckle until the post is aligned and the gate operates freely.

To bring a leaning hinge post back into plumb, attach a sag rod. Sag rods are typically sold as kits that include a pair of threaded rods, a turnbuckle, and fastening hardware. Correct leaning fence posts as shown in the drawing, with the upper end of the rod attached to the upper end of the sagging post. Tighten the turnbuckle on the rod until the post is plumb.

Reinforcing Gate Posts

If the posts are sound but simply loose or unstable in the ground, reinforce them with concrete.

1 Aligning the Posts. Dig a trench between the gate posts as wide and deep as the postholes. If the posts are not set in concrete, also dig around the post perimeters to add a concrete collar. Once the trench is dug, force the posts back into alignment and brace temporarily.

2 Adding Gravel Base. Backfill the trench with 3 to 4 inches of compacted gravel or crushed rock.

3 Placing Concrete. Backfill the remainder of the trench with concrete, until the concrete is level with the ground.

1 Dig between and around sagging gate posts before forcing them back into alignment.

2 Pour 3 to 4 in. of gravel into the trench and holes.

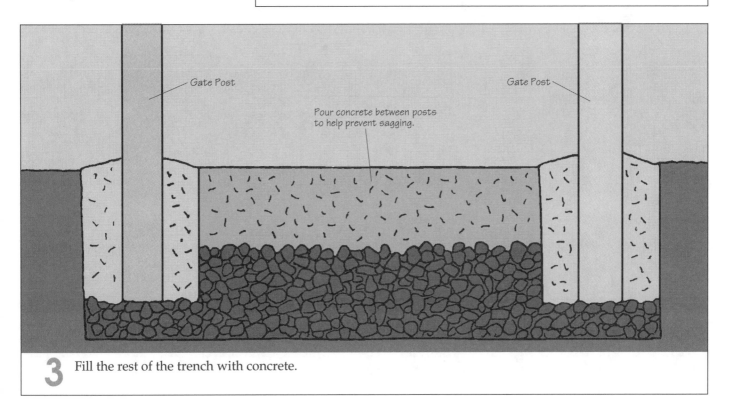

Gate Post

Gate Post

Pour concrete between posts to help prevent sagging.

3 Fill the rest of the trench with concrete.

Reinforcing a Gate Frame

Sometimes the gate frame itself may be the cause of binding. If the hinges are tight, and the posts are plumb, make sure the gate is square. An out-of-square or racked gate may require bracing. If the gate-frame connections are weak, they'll need to be reinforced with either a plywood gusset or metal bracket.

1 Reinforcing the Joints. If the gate structure is weak, you can reinforce the corner joints. First pull the gate into square. To do this, measure the diagonals of the frame. Run a clamp along the long diagonal, and tighten gently until the diagonals are the same length. Reinforce the gate with a metal bracket or plywood gusset. Fasten any loose boards or siding with galvanized deck screws.

2 Adding Diagonal Bracing. To prevent further sagging, attach a sag rod between the top of the hinge side and the bottom of the latch side. You can also add a diagonal wood brace, if the gate doesn't already have one. (See "Bracing the Frame," page 62.) Unlike sag rods, wood braces are installed with the high end on the latch side and the low end on the hinge side.

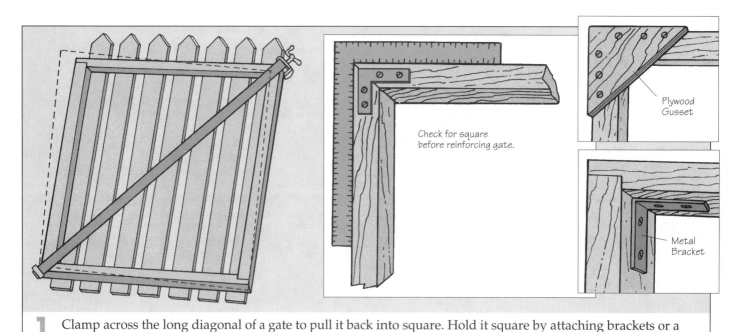

Check for square before reinforcing gate.

Plywood Gusset

Metal Bracket

1 Clamp across the long diagonal of a gate to pull it back into square. Hold it square by attaching brackets or a plywood gusset.

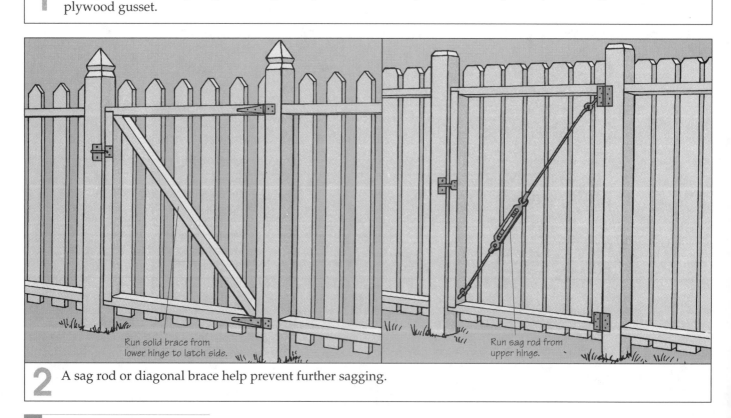

Run solid brace from lower hinge to latch side.

Run sag rod from upper hinge.

2 A sag rod or diagonal brace help prevent further sagging.

Arbor Garden structure that can support plants and serves as a transition between sections of a yard or as an architectural feature that complements the landscape.

Backfill Sand, dirt, gravel, or crushed stone used to fill the space around an excavation area.

Battens Strips of wood placed over or between fence posts.

Batter boards Boards used to support strings that mark the position of a fence at the start of construction.

Blind corner Created when a fence is built on a corner lot and obstructs views at an intersection or sharp bend in the road.

Board foot A measurement of wood by volume; each board foot is equivalent to one square foot at one inch of thickness.

Bracing Wood member used to support a structure. In fence building, bracing is usually only temporarily.

Caster A wheel installed at the bottom of a gate to prevent sagging.

Chain link fence Prefabricated fence consisting of metal poles and chain link mesh. These fences are durable and provide good security, but no privacy.

Clamshell digger A hand tool composed of two hinged, shovel-like parts that loosen soil and then grasp it for removal from postholes.

Concrete collar A ring of concrete placed around posts to securely anchor them; also prevents water from collecting around the posts.

Dado A rectangular groove cut at a right angle to the grain of a wood. Dadoes are most often used in joinery to receive another piece of wood.

Diagonal-board gate In this type of gate, boards are placed on an angle to give the gate extra strength without additional bracing.

Fiberglass panel A substitute for plywood or plastic fence panels, these panels are either flat or corrugated and admit light while obscuring views.

Frost line The maximum depth to which soil freezes in winter. Your local building department can provide information of the frost-line depth in your area below which posts must be placed to prevent heaving.

Galvanized nail Exterior nail that is coated with zinc to prevent rusting.

Gate spring A device with a long, heavy spring and two brackets or eye screws that shuts a gate automatically.

Gate strike A piece attached to either side of the fence and to either the post or the gate. It keeps the gate from swinging past its closure point and bending the hinges.

Kickboard A 1x8 or 1x10 piece installed along the bottom of the posts to strengthen a fence and prevent animals from crawling underneath.

Lattice Thin strips of wood that are crossed to make a pattern for a trellis or an arbor.

Louver fence A fence with boards installed either vertically or horizontally on an angle so that they serve as filters for wind and sunlight.

Penny Unit of measurement (noted d) for nail length, such as a 10d nail, which is 3 inches long.

Plumb Vertically straight.

Post Vertical framing member such as a 4x4 or 4x6, set in the ground to support a fence.

Post-and-rail fence Fence with posts that have one, two, or three rails toe-nailed or dadoed into them.

Power auger A gas-powered tool used for drilling into the ground. Often rented by homeowners to dig multiple postholes.

Pressure-treated wood Wood that has preservatives forced into it under pressure to repel rot and insects.

Prefabricated fence Fence made with posts and panels that are prefabricated of wood, metal, or PVC plastic and come ready to assemble.

Property-line fence Fence that is centered directly on the property line, meaning that tenants on both sides share ownership.

Rail Horizontal framing member, usually a 2x4 or 2x6, to which the fence boards are attached.

Sag rod A rod or cable with an adjustable turnbuckle that is used like a wood brace to keep gates from sagging.

Segmented fence A fence consisting of short, straight sections attached to posts plotted along a curve.

Spacer board A board ripped to the width between pickets that is used to make even spaces on a fence.

Trellis An open-framed garden structure on which plants and vines can grow.

Utility fencing Narrow wood slats held together with wire, sold in large rolls that are nailed to permanent or temporary wood or metal posts.

Vertical board-on-board fence Fence that is fully sided to provide privacy while not entirely blocking sunlight.

Vinyl fence Prefabricated fence made of PVC plastic that imitates a variety of fence designs, including board, rail, picket, lattice, and ornamental metal.

Welded wire Woven wire mesh that is often attached to a wood fence to act as a trellis for climbing vines.

Wire picket fencing Rolls of factory-painted or vinyl-coated welded-wire fencing that come in heights of 12 to 18 inches.

Wood-and-wire fence Welded or woven-wire mesh that is attached to a wood frame to make a lightweight, economical fence.

Z-brace gate A reinforced gate with a Z-shaped wood brace found on a solid-board fence, a masonry wall, or a breezeway between buildings.

- Alternating panel fence, 34–35
  Angled post top, 28–30

- Backfilling, 20, 22
  Battens, adding, 46
  Board fences, 24, 26–28
  Board foot, 9
  Board-top variations, 26
  Borate-treated lumber, 8
  Braces, installing, 63–64
  Building codes, 9–10

- Cap rail, 28–30, 32
  Casters, 60
  CCA pressure-treated wood, 6
  Center support, 32
  Chain fences, 56
  Chain link fences, 6, 53–56
  Chamfered post top, 28–30
  Clamshell digger, 6
  Concrete, backfilling with, 20
  Corner boards, attaching, 31
  Corners, establishing additional, 12
  Creosote, 8
  Cross braces, 66
  Curved-top picket fence, 39

- Decay resistance in lumber, 6, 8
  Diagonal-board gate, 64–65
  Diagonal bracing, 78
  Dust mask, 6

- Earth, tamping, 19
  End posts, 12, 18, 21

- Fence plotting, 12–13, 15–18
  Fence-height laws, 9
  Fence line, 6, 15
  Fences
     board, 24, 26–28, 31–32
     board-on-board, 33–37
     chain, 56
     chain link, 53–56
     cleaning, 72–73
     curved, 25
     lattice-top, 36–37
     louver, 35–36
     maintaining, 71–73
     ornamental metal, 48–50
     picket, 37–40, 56
     plotting, 12–13, 15–18
     plywood, 44–45
     post-and-board, 42–46
     post-and-rail, 40–41, 42
     prefab, 24, 48–50
     property-line, 26
     repairing, 73–78
     rope, 56

     segmented, 25
     on slope, 13, 15–18
     solid-board privacy, 30–31
     utility, 56
     vinyl, 50–52
     wood-and-wire, 45–46
  Fiberglass, 44
  Finish, 70–71
  Frost heave, 10
  Frost line, 10

- Gate-on-frame, 61–63
  Gates
     diagonal-board, 64–65
     direction of swing, 58–59
     fixing sagging, 76
     hardware for, 59–60
     installing, 56, 68
     lattice-and-board, 67–68
     picket, 65–67
     reinforcing, 77, 78
     selecting location, 58
     size and weight, 58
     wooden, 61–68
     Z-brace, 63–64
  Gate strike, 63
  Gravel fill, 19

- Half-lap joint, 66
  Hand auger, 6
  Hinges, 59, 68, 76
  Horizontal board fences, 31–32

- Kickboards, 29–30, 32

- Latch bar, 61
  Latches, 59–60, 61, 68
  Lattice-and-board gate, 67–68
  Lattice-top fence, 36–37
  Layout and digging tools, 6, 7
  Level line, 16
  Locks, 59
  Louver fences, 35–36
  Lumber, 6, 8–9

- Mason's twine, 6, 12

- Neighborhood restrictions, 9
  90-degree corner, 12

- Obstacles, dealing with, 14
  Ornamental metal fences, 48–50

- Paint, 70
  Panels, 44
  Picket fences, 37–40
  Picket gate, 65–67
  Plumb bob, 6
  Plywood fence, 44–45

- Post-and-board fence, 42–46
  Post-and-rail fence, 40–41, 42
  Postholes, 6, 19, 48–49, 54
  Post pickets, 39
  Posts
     bracing, 20–21
     checking alignment, 72
     dadoing, 29
     installing, 18–21, 51
     joining rails to, 28–30
     locations for, 12–17
     mortising, 41
     repairing, 73–77
     setting, 17, 18, 19, 21, 22, 49, 54
  Prefab fences, 9, 24, 48–50
  Pressure-treated wood, 70
  Property-line fences, 26

- Rails
     attaching, 28–30, 32
     preventing sagging, 29
     repairing, 72, 75
  Reed and bamboo screening, 56
  Rope fences, 56
  Rot, checking for, 71–72

- Sag rods, 60
  Screws, tightening loose, 76
  Segmented fences, 25
  Siding, repairing, 72, 75
  Slope, fences on, 13, 15–18
  Solid-board privacy fence, 30–31
  Spacer, making, 36
  Springs, 60
  Stains, 70
  Step heights, marking, 17
  Stepped footing forms, 14
  Step size, determining, 17

- Tenons, cutting, in rails, 41

- Utilities, locating, 10
  Utility fencing, 56
  U.V. blocker, 8

- Varnishes, 70
  Vertical board-on-board fence, 33–37
  Vinyl-coated wire, 45
  Vinyl fences, 50–52

- Water sealer, 70
  Welded wire, 45
  Wire picket fencing, 56
  Wood-and-wire fence, 45–46
  Wooden gate, 61–68

- Z-brace gate, 63–64
  Zoning laws, 9